Apocapiphany

by

Helen Van Dahl

This book is dedicated to Helen.

Helen is not me.

She represents my Mother, my Grandmother, My Sister, My Auntie, my best friend and every single woman who's ever been abused by a man, or men, or even a group of men purporting to be servants of God, and survived to tell her tale. Sadly all too many "Helens" do not survive.

All names have been changed to protect the innocent, and in many cases, the guilty too.

Chapters

1. How do
2. Home Farm
3. Hatred
4. Horrible Happenings
5. Hallelujah!
6. Horny
7. Hallucinating
8. Homeless
9. Huntin' Hounds
10. Horny part II
11. Horses
12. Hormones
13. Hypnagogic
14. Hard Work
15. Happy Couples?
16. Hospital
17. Heaven or Hell?
18. Healing
19. Hovis Biscuits
20. Hateful ~~Eight, Ten,~~ Nine
21. Horny Part III
22. Happily Ever After?
23. Hamburg

Glossary of JW Terms

Suggested Reading / Viewing

Chapter One

"How Do"

This popular Yorkshire greeting has a silent "H" and should really be pronounced "Ow doo" but in the spirit of this book, rules are made to be broken.

I spent most of my childhood on a remote Yorkshire farm and as a result, had a strong Yorkshire accent until I was around 9 or 10 years old. A lot of people don't know this about me as I now have a very strong Scottish accent. When my parents moved to Scotland in the early 80's I found it very difficult to understand what everyone was saying and vice versa. For about the first year or so following the move, most of my childhood interactions with anyone outwith my immediate family consisted of "What?" and "Eh?"

I really should have been more politely spoken after all - I was brought up to be. It should have been "Pardon me"? and "Sorry I didn't quite catch that, could you repeat it please"? but when frustration with your limited ability to grasp the local dialect begins to brew, the words become more guttural. In the end I realised these new friends and neighbours were not going to adapt their speech to suit me, therefore I was going to have to adapt mine to suit them. Thus began the lengthy process of me attempting to speak in a Scottish accent whilst simultaneously attempting to rid myself of my coarse Yorkshire one. It took about 2 years to complete the process, much to the amusement of my school friends who laughed at my Mel Gibson-like early attempts. My family, on the other hand, thought I was a little traitor for dropping my roots so quickly. After all my Dad was a proud Yorkshireman and my Grandad also, he was born at Malham Cove and apparently you don't get much more Yorkshireish than that. My Great Grandfather was a Scotsman though so I clung to that, and a rebellious wee Scotswoman was what I was determined to be. Even if every time my elderly Grandparents would ring I slipped back into my old accent on the phone, or if Mum was giving me a scolding for something a few old words would pop out here and there and mess up my newfound Scottish lilt.

To this day though, I'm the only "Scottish" member of my family, which has an iconic Scottish name and I'm quite proud of that. It shows my ability to adapt to new surroundings, to negotiate and barter to make life easier both for myself and those around me, and of course that thing which is so essential for surviving childhood and young adulthood : conformity and being able to "Fit in"

The farm in Yorkshire holds many memories and many secrets though. Some remain locked away forever in a deep, dark Pandora's box I have chosen not to open. They are not secrets of my own making, not choices I was old enough to choose or paths I was conscious of walking, but instead a dark pit of unknown silence which I am happy to keep the lid on. Some things you are simply best not knowing! The brain is a marvellous organ, capable of shutting out immense pain and emotion, things too bleak to bear, too confusing to understand, too awful to fully comprehend. We can store them deep somewhere within a compartment only regression hypnotherapy could probably access and I'm thankful for this. I will now tell the tale of the memories I do recall and as time goes on I piece them together. With the help of my Sister I make sense of some of them. Others make no sense and memories fade over time, merging with vivid dreams where you awaken asking "Did that really happen"? I think this too is a cushioning mechanism of the brain, designed to protect us from the traumas which haunt us the most. Fading them from sharp, raw, jagged edges into soft, blurry, hazy out of focus pictures, growing dimmer over time.

Chapter Two

Home Farm

Childhood memories are a strange entity. I'm always amazed when I hear of people who can recount their earliest experiences, being bathed in the sink aged 1, what kind of teddy bear they slept with in their cot or parasol they had over their pram as their Mother pushed them around in it. No such clarity for me! My first memory is of waking up sharply, as though from a bad dream, feeling the gasp of cold air as I inhaled, and watching the cloud of white vapour erupt from my mouth, filling the icy caravan as I exhaled. I looked down at my mittens which were frozen to my fingers, possibly from me trying to suck my thumb or bite my nails during the night. I was fully clothed and under thick blankets but oh my God it was cold in that caravan! I was about 3 or 4 years old and I remember feeling afraid that the cold was going to consume me, gripping my tiny bones and turning them into shards of ice. My sister is asleep next to me, on waking she offered both words of comfort and warmth from a hug.

My parents, having watched one too many episodes of "The Good Life" decided to move from Sussex to remote rural North Yorkshire and in the late 70's they bought a derelict farmhouse and barn with a somewhat chequered history. It had been left to rack and ruin, squatted in by some hippies who were subsequently evicted and then burned the place down in retribution. Then to put the cherry on the cake, a nasty gangland argument went awry one fateful night and a man was murdered and buried in the garden. I suspect this sequence of unfortunate events led to my parents being able to purchase said farm at a significantly reduced price. Although back then a four figure sum would still have been a considerable investment.

Their plan was to live in the caravan whilst my Dad built one of the byres into a bedroom - come dining room, then when that was complete we would move in there while he converted the rest of the house, leaving the caravan for two of my older brothers. The other two had the sense to flee the nest well before this move.

One of my next clear memories jumps forward in time to when we're now living, eating and sleeping cramped into the partially converted byre and I remember being afraid. The source of my fear was having to pass the bed where my Dad was sleeping in order to use the toilet. I remember holding it in for as long as possible, and even contemplating wetting the bed, something I'd never done, rather than have to get up in the freezing cold and walk past that awful man, but eventually the pain from my bladder and common sense prevailed. I had no choice but to creep hastily across the arctic floor to the relief the toilet offered.

You may ask why did I feel so afraid of him? what had he done to me to make me feel this way? These are good questions and if asked, right at that moment in time, I would have no solid answer for. You can decide for yourself as you keep reading. Your guess could be as good as mine. You can feel free to decide what grim fate you think befell me before the morning I woke up in the cold caravan.

A Psychologist would many years later scrawl "UNKNOWN CHILDHOOD TRAUMA, POSSIBLE ABUSE? " into her notes and the full stop at the end of the question mark is where I'm happy to leave the matter. I just remember hating everything about him. His voice, his smell - stale tobacco breath and greasy hair, his look, the way he could walk into a room and immediately command it, making everyone present feel uneasy and unhappy in equal measures.

Alongside these, and other memories tinged with fear, are thankfully many happy ones. Growing up on a farm in the middle of nowhere, down a wee winding lane isolated from the world, can be a very healthy way to spend your childhood. When I see children today glued to their electronic devices I feel sorry they are missing out on some of the experiences I had. Most of my happy memories are of times spent with my older sister Kate. Playing together by the river, skimming stones, climbing trees, larking around and generally trying to forget all about the bad stuff which ran parallel to our idyllic life. The wilderness was our sanctuary, the trees our confidants we whispered our secrets to as we sat within their branches. The beck out back was our happy place, the sound of the water tumbling over the stones helped to drown out the bad thoughts and feelings in our minds, at least for a time anyway. I remember making hay in old fashioned "stooks" with wooden rakes and the smell of it drying in the sun. I don't think I've ever smelt hay as good as those stooks. How good it felt to slide into bed at night tired and sore from hard work, but satisfied from spending all day outdoors, working together the way families did for thousands of years before industry and heavy machinery really took over. I remember lying in the cut hay fields after the stooks had been lifted, again with my older sister, my best friend in the whole world, we lay on our backs and watched the clouds roll across the sky above us. "Look! That one looks a bit like a horse"

"No it doesn't it's more like a cow"

"Look at that one over there it looks like Uncle Fred with his big whisky nose" and we would burst into laughter and watch them until they turned red. Then sadness began to creep in as we knew eventually we had to return to the farm house.

It's hard even now all these years later to write anything good about my Father but if forced to, if made to say just one thing that was honourable about him it was that farm house. He built it stone by stone, hours of laborious blood, sweat and tears and what a beautiful house it was when it was finished. Beautiful on the outside, full of ugliness and anger on the inside. Shouting, arguing, smashed cups and plates, punched holes in doors, and other moments which didn't make any sense until many years later when I pieced them together like a fragmented jigsaw

It sold recently for a million pounds and is the highest priced house in the entire area. It's the one thing, aside from fathering my brother Lloyd and I that I can honestly say he did well.

Aside from that, I'd be clutching at straws to say anything kinder. Mum always defended him saying he was a hard worker and a breadwinner, putting food on our table and clothes on our backs. I suppose I can't argue with that. He did provide financially for us, but that was all the positivity I can remember him contributing.

Chapter Three

Hatred

I remember the first time I felt hatred brewing in my heart. I was around 4 or 5 years old and we had a pigsty on the opposite side of the courtyard to the farmhouse. I was sitting on the wall alongside the sty, watching my Father working on the slate roof of the house and I became consumed with the feeling of intense hatred, thinking I wished, or hoped that he would slide off the roof and that would be the end of him. I remember my heart pounding inside my little chest, knowing it was wrong to be thinking this and if it actually did happen would it be because I had caused it to? Would that make me a murderer like in the films I'd secretively seen on the telly when I wasn't meant to be watching? A small flock of pigeons disturbed by his activity erupted out of the eaves from the byre next door, flying high and away. I focussed intently on them instead because even though I was very young, I knew you weren't supposed to think these kind of thoughts. I didn't know why I was having them, or how to make them stop. I just knew I needed to find a way to make sure I had as little to do with him as possible so I wouldn't need to think them. So I tried to avoid looking at him, talking to him or having any form of interaction whatsoever unless it was absolutely necessary.

Things like mealtimes or journeys in the van were the worst. We'd go through this seemingly endless ritual of my Dad asking me something like "Are you OK?" me refusing to answer or acknowledge him, and then Mum interjecting that I needed to show my Father respect when he was talking to me by answering him. I would usually try to give the shortest grunt possible to make him stop looking at, or talking to me. An argument of some kind would then take place between them, always instigated by my Dad and usually ending with Mum falling silent also.

I vividly recall an assignment at Primary School where we had to draw a picture of our Dad and write a bit about him. My Dad was a mining manager so I drew him with his yellow hard hat, blue overalls, big angry face and his bushy beard. I wrote that my Dad was the angry man in the yellow hat who came home from work and threw things at my Mum. I wonder what on earth my teacher thought? I don't remember my drawing ever being on the wall beside the other children proudly showing off their nice Dads. But to me that's just who he was. He'd come storming in the door, like an angry whirlwind and anything my Mum said to him would make him angrier. It would usually culminate in shouting and him throwing his dinner at the wall next to Mum. As far as I'm aware he never actually hit her? If he did I never saw him do it. The threat was always there though. As much as there was relief when he left the room after his violent tantrums, there was always sadness for Mum as she quietly got up and swept up the mess and then tried to make sure everyone else ate their dinner despite what had just happened.

I think I was around 6 or 7? When My brother Lloyd gave me a present of a diary. I'd never had one and wasn't sure what to write in it, so I just started to write how I felt. It was a small book filled with big hate. Pages and pages of how much I hated him, often in capital letters for emphasis. Sometimes I hated Mum too for being married to him and not shouting back or making him leave, so I'd write that I hated her too even though it was always temporary, I loved her really. Eventually I wrote **I HATE EVERYONE!!!!!**

One day, it was bound to happen of course, Mum found the diary. Understandably she was really upset. I did feel bad, I told her I was sorry for writing about her in it, I genuinely hadn't meant it, it was only my Dad I hated. She told me I wasn't to hate him, he was my Father and I was to respect him. The diary was taken away. It was my only means of venting, clever little thing that I was, my own self-help therapist at such a young age. I wasn't sure what I was supposed to do with these feelings now I couldn't write them in the diary and lock it, put it in the drawer and try to forget about it all.

It didn't help that Mum showed me a photo of me from before the move, in our old back yard in Sussex with my Dad. I remember being shocked to the core to see it. He was smiling and holding me close, I was smiling too, what on earth was going on? I tried to reason surely this wasn't me wasn't it my brother? Was Mum trying to trick me in some way? No, it was definitely me, I recognised the back yard from other photos and myself from the rest of the pictures in the same sequence. I felt strange. Now as an adult, I fully comprehend what it was I felt, it was disgust.

I was also angrier than ever, the hatred raged inside me, coursed through my veins and filled up every part of me until I wanted to explode. I had to find a new way to get rid of this unpleasant feeling, so I would go down to the railway tunnel near our farm and scream at the top of my lungs as the trains went past. Somehow I instinctively knew that screaming without the trains to drown it out would cause me problems. It would be something else I'd be found out for, told off for and banned from doing, so this became my new way to release it without anyone knowing. Except it only worked for a while and then I needed something more to quell the storm inside so one day, not quite knowing why, I decided to bite down hard on my arm instead, and that definitely helped. The pain seemed to rush to my arm soothing, distracting me from and calming the rage inside me. However, I bit so hard I broke the skin and left teeth marks.

Now I had something new and more awkward to hide from Mum. This was more difficult than the diary which to be fair, I did a rubbish job of concealing. Naively I thought it was my private diary and Mum would never seek out the key and read it. I didn't manage to hide my new therapy habit for long! Despite wearing long sleeves and pulling them down to cover it, she soon spotted the vampiristic tooth prints and asked aghast, who had done this to me? I reluctantly confessed it was me and received a severe telling off for it, made to promise never to do that ever again. It was a hard promise to keep, I'd only just discovered something that helped alleviate how I was feeling, but somehow I managed to squish the feelings down and subdue them. We were soon going to be moving to Scotland and my Dad would be working a different job where he would be at home much less so this gave me a hope to look forward to that maybe, just maybe things might be different, less shouting and broken things.

At this point he was starting to terrorise Kate too. I remember the time she came rushing into my room and breathlessly told me to lock the door. No matter what happened on the other side of it, not to let him in. He came bawling and banging on the door but we stayed firmly put, except now Kate had gone from being panicky and out of breath to hyperventilating and turning pale. I was torn between hatred of him and concern for her, and eventually when she began gasping and nodded her head, I let him in. I was ushered out of the way so I'm hazy on what happened next but I know a doctor arrived. I remember she had to blow into a tube or bag of some kind to bring her breathing back to normal. She left home not long after this and I never saw her for many years. I think we all hoped the move to Scotland would be a new beginning. For me it was the beginning of things becoming far worse.

Chapter Four

Horrible Happenings

"Thump......Thump.....Thump" went the rhythmic noise. At first faint and muffled, but then for some reason my heart seemed to be beating in unison with the sound making it unbearable to listen to any longer.

"Thump......thump.....thump"

It was coming from the living room downstairs, directly below my bedroom and without knowing why, I sensed this ominous sound was something awful occurring. I also felt compelled to go downstairs and see what was making it. Not only did I urgently need the toilet now in a fight or flight like response but something in my gut told me nobody else in the house could stop it. The downstairs living room was his room in the evenings after Mum had gone to bed. It was his grotty drinking den where he watched films, sometimes ranted to himself and often fell asleep fat, snoring and dishevelled in the chair. If you've ever watched Father Ted you'll probably think of the chair Father Jack sat in and you wouldn't be far off the mark. It was the only room with a TV, during the daytime Mum would watch her soap operas there with a nice fire blazing. It was a welcoming and cosy room then, but the minute that bastard came home from work the entire atmosphere of the room, and indeed house, changed to a sinister one.

I didn't want to go down but something told me if I didn't my Mum might not survive. The moment I woke I thought "My Dad's murdering my Mum down there!" Which really, years later when I think about it, doesn't make sense as if he were, you'd think there would be screaming or a more random pattern to the sounds. No, being realistic, even as young as I was I think I knew deep down that wasn't exactly what was happening, I just knew it was something bad and it needed to stop.

As I opened the door my pounding heart had reached a crescendo where I felt almost lightheaded, perhaps because as I passed the kitchen on the way to the living room I felt a strong urge to go to the cutlery drawer and arm myself with a knife, a big one, to defend myself, my Mother or anyone else who happened to need it.

The scene which awaited me when I turned the handle and walked in was my father on his knees in front of his grotty armchair having perverted sex with an underage, non-consenting minor. He looked up and instantly stopped what he was doing, pushed them away from him and zipped up his trousers, then sat back in the chair looking at the floor as though nothing had happened. I didn't really know how to process this, so I rushed to the toilet my head whizzing at a hundred miles per hour.

As I sat there, shaking, trying to process what I'd just seen I asked myself "Is this real? Am I sleepwalking?" I pinched myself to make sure, "Ow, that hurt, Ok so this is really happening" "Fuuuuuuuuuck!!!"

I heard him leave the living room and go into his "junkshop" which was an outhouse where he liked to pile up completely useless stuff to the ceiling as he was an obsessive hoarder. The moment I heard the door close I knew I was safe to make a run for the stairs to my Mum's room to tell her.

I hurriedly woke her, told her in the most straightforward terms what I'd just caught him doing, the words sounding alien and contrived as they came out of my mouth. I then begged her to please, please, please get him out of the house. I offered to call the Police if he refused as I knew this act was criminally wrong as well as morally.

Obviously Mum was disorientated and shocked but I stood triumphantly with her at the top of the stairs while she shouted down to him to come out and face her, thinking to myself "Yes, oh yes, please let this be the day we get rid of him for GOOD!" but it didn't quite play out like that. She asked him if it was true, he was playing the meek little boy act looking ashamedly down at the floor. He admitted yes it was true. I started yelling all sorts of expletives that had been brewing since the times in Yorkshire when I used to scream at the trains only now I was older, I knew the right words to go with the yells. Neither my Mother or Father had ever heard language like that come out of my mouth as it was a strict household and a religious one too. But out they came, streaming into the air turning it blue. "You dirty fucking bastard" "How could you do that? Your disgusting you fucking PAEDO, get the fuck out of this house"

To my horror my Mum turned to me and told me to stop using bad language and that we would sort this out in the morning, for tonight he would sleep in the downstairs bedroom, I was outraged at this, as he had been sleeping here for some months anyway since their marriage was on the rocks. So his "punishment" was to sleep where he normally slept anyway? It was raining and I thought how nice would it be for him to have to sleep outside in the pissing rain all night with no socks or shoes on, exactly the same way he made my brother sleep outside in his underpants one night he came home drunk. I was only small at the time but I remember waking up to the strong stench of fresh puke and my Dad yelling at my brother that if he was going to treat this house like a pig sty then he could spend the night outside with the pigs in the actual pig sty. I'll never forget feeling sorry for him as I looked out the window and saw him shivering, pale and cold in just his Y fronts. I thought to myself "You horrible Bastard" about my Dad back then but I didn't know those were the words to go with the emotion. It seemed only fitting that my Mum banishing him to the same fate was the minimum justice to be served that night until the Police came. But no, Mum insisted he go to his room, like a petulant school child given a slap on the wrist, I should spend the night in her bed with her so I would be safe and we would sort it all out tomorrow.

I didn't get much sleep that night, I cried, Mum cried, I felt dirty, angry, humiliated and vengeful. It felt as though he had done something vile to me without even touching me. I don't know what emotions my Mum felt but I suspect all of them to some degree except her strict religious beliefs would likely kick in and prevent the vengeful one from becoming too prominent. Christians must forgive, they must turn the other cheek after all. This felt rather more of a blow to the guts than a slap to the face though!

Mum summoned "The Elders" who duly came for a meeting, a sombre looking group of stern men in suits. We sat around the kitchen table, Mum looking mortified, my Dad the quietest I've ever seen him, staring sheepishly at the floor and me, heart pounding in my chest awaiting them saying something like he must come with them to the Police Station or leave the house. I was half nervous - half excited at the prospect of him finally getting the eviction he deserved. I was determined to do whatever I could during the meeting to ensure this outcome.

To my complete disgust and dismay they did nothing of the kind!

They read a couple of scriptures from Leviticus and Deuteronomy covering the sin my Father had committed then asked him how he felt about it. He never broke his gaze from the floor as he said quietly that he regretted it and was very sorry. In my head I was shouting "Liar! he was only sorry he got caught, more like!" But the Elders were to be respected so I waited my turn. They asked me what I thought about the scriptures they had read. I spoke up, heart pounding like a crazy jungle drum, knowing this was my one and only chance to get my views across. I said that I wholeheartedly agreed that he should be stoned to death, but not his victim as it wasn't their fault he was a disgusting pervert. The Elders explained that we no longer live in those times and stoning people to death wasn't a viable punishment option. I said "OK let's call the Police and let them deal with him instead then!"

They turned back to my parents and began reading more scriptures, this time about repentance and forgiveness. I honestly couldn't believe the utter tripe I was hearing and sat there furious, the feelings continuing long after they picked up their Bibles and briefcases and left.

I was filled with a rage like never before. I tried to talk to Mum about it but she said the matter was closed. It was in God's hands now and not for us to meddle with. Besides, bringing it out into the open with anyone other than the Elders would bring reproach on God's name. I wasn't to tell anyone, call anyone or do anything.

I couldn't stop thinking about that big knife in the drawer and what could have happened if I'd gone there first before opening the door? Might I have had the courage to plunge it deep into that horrible fat belly of his and dish out some justice of my own? It wasn't a thought I wanted to think but I found myself consumed by it. The whole horrible scenario was to replay in my mind over and over again for many years afterwards. Each time it replayed I went to the kitchen and got the knife. Sometimes I burst in through the door and threatened him out of the house with it and called the Police, sometimes I stabbed him with it, other times I just stood there in the kitchen and listened to the sound of my pounding heart before going back to bed and deciding not to open the door after all. No matter how hard I tried I never did manage to replay it where I was ever able to get there first and stop the incident from happening.

Each time I replayed it I felt the same emotions, disgust, annoyance, disappointment in myself for not having done something, anything, more than I did which was close the door and go to the toilet without saying a word, but I realise now I was in shock. When we're in shock we don't always do or say the things we would if we had time to prepare beforehand.

Most of the trauma which followed in my adult life stemmed from this one incident. Not just the witnessing of it and being unable to do anything to prevent it or change it but on a much deeper level of emotional hurt, the sheer betrayal and let-down I experienced at the hands of my Mum's handling of the whole matter. I've since managed to understand and forgive her actions, for her life wasn't her own you see. Not only was she trapped in an abusive marriage, she was also involved with a domineering, controlling and coercive religious cult, which I had been instrumental in unwittingly reintroducing her to!

Chapter 5

HalleluJah!

I'm around 11 years old and in Primary school, I have a friend called Stu who's in first year of High School. He was a quiet kid, didn't seem to have many friends and lived in the house at the top of the hill with his Dad who had recently separated from his Mum. One day when we were playing in the street on our bikes, Stu fell from his onto the road and started crying, the other kids began teasing him, calling him "gay" and a "wimp" which of course only made him cry all the more. After everyone else rode off I went over to see if he was OK, feeling sorry for him I helped him up. We got chatting and from there a friendship was forged, albeit a brief one.

One day not long after the bike incident, Stu gave me a magazine. He said he was sure I'd find it really interesting, one article in particular was all about dogs, which was, is and always will be one of my favourite subjects to read or talk about. Looking back it was crafty the way he conveniently folded the pages of the magazine over to reveal just the dog related article so that I'd read it, enjoy it and then turn to the other pages afterwards. The magazine was called "Awake" and being an avid bookworm, I devoured the dog article then went on to read the magazine in its entirety. Stu had asked me for feedback so the next time I saw him I said how much I'd enjoyed it and he gave me a book this time. A burgundy one with an embossed cover and an intriguing title :

"You can live forever in Paradise on Earth"

Well doesn't that sound peachy! Who wouldn't want to immediately open up a book which promises you something like that?

Of course none of this was a coincidence, Stu and his father were Jehovah's Witnesses and I was later to discover, they attended weekly meetings with the sole aim of instructing them on the best, most effective and strategic ways to preach to people, including what's known as "Informal Witnessing" This is where Jehovah's Witnesses use normal everyday settings to try to strike up conversations or place literature with friends, neighbours, family, co-workers or anyone they might come across outwith the traditional door-to-door ministry most people associate them with. I have to hand it to them, it's a cunning approach.

If your doorbell rings on a Saturday morning and you peek through the curtains or blinds and spot two men in suits carrying briefcases, you're automatically going to assume they are selling something. And you wouldn't be wrong in this case! Eternal salvation comes at a price you know. A friendly chat on the other hand, this can be disarming, catching you off guard as you don't expect the religious content.

However, back to the book :

Released in 1982 the "Paradise Book" as it commonly came to be known, was used as a Bible study aid for Jehovah's Witnesses to recruit and indoctrinate new members. In its initial release 5,000,000 copies were released. By the year 1989 72,600,000 copies were printed. When I was given a copy by Stu I had no idea what it was about but happily took it off home and read it from cover to cover. It seemed to make a lot of sense to me! I liked the idea of there being a reason for all the awful things that were happening in the world, according to this book it wasn't actually meant to be this way! There was something we could do to find a way out of this mess into a wonderful new world. I loved the artwork, all the happy faces, beautiful gardens, friendly animals, stunning homes. Everyone seemed to be enjoying life aged to around somewhere in their late 20's to early 30's, without any physical imperfection or health impediment, having the chance to live that way for all eternity. Who wouldn't want to sign up to that when the daily news was full of wars, starving Ethiopian babies crying with their tiny little spindly arms outstretched begging for food. Flies landing on their cracked, dry mouths and crawling across their pot bellies. Who wouldn't want a world with no poverty, hatred, crime and illness?

I told Mum about the book, if I remember rightly I raved about how good it was and how she should read it. She didn't say much if anything about it at all and I popped the book on the shelf awaiting Stu's next offering, which was never to come as shortly afterwards he and his Dad moved away.

Some months later I woke one night to Mum shining a torch along the huge bookcase beside my bed.

"Mum it's the middle of the night, what on earth are you doing"? I asked quizzically.

"I'm looking for that book"

"Which book?"

"The Paradise one, you know the one I mean!"

I fetched the book for her and got back into
bed. I don't even think she thanked me, she
wandered out of my room silently just holding
and staring at it transfixed, like someone who
had found the Holy Grail (pun fully intended)

I didn't give it too much thought but then Mum
seemed to have some kind of really deep,
intense mental breakdown and ended up in
hospital. As well as being a really worrying time
this was also a time in my life which really
impacted on me as I was sent off to stay with a
friend and finally got to see what an actual
"normal" family looked like. How they interacted
with each other and a glimpse of what life was
supposed to look like. It was both refreshing
and crushing at the same time. Refreshing
because it gave me hope that I was right to feel
my home environment was NOT normal or
healthy. Crushing because I realised I was never
going to see scenes like I had at my friend's
house, a loving husband laughing, joking and
showing affection to his wife or a brother and

sister teasing each other in fun and jest. The love between the members of this family was palpable. Part of me missed Mum and was worried sick about her, the other part of me longed for this glimpse of a better life and didn't want to go home.

Finally she was released from hospital and as much as I couldn't stand my Dad, not wanting anything to do with him, even before the horrible happenings incident had happened, we were forced to have "a talk about your Mother"

He explained that Mum had experienced some kind of religious epiphany and was from now on going to become a Jehovah's Witness again. I replied "Woah, hang on what do you mean AGAIN?"

So, it turns out Mum had been a baptised Jehovah's Witness years before I arrived on the scene. She was in her previous unhappy marriage and had taken vows to serve God, but then my Dad came along, younger, more charming, handsome and offering my Mum the sun moon and stars to go off with him, which she did, thus breaking her vows to her God in the process.

Jehovah's Witness protocol for any person who abandons their marriage and lives in sin with someone else is a process called "Disfellowshipping" If you are considered to be unrepentant i.e. not sorry for all the great, hot sex you are getting with your new man, you are then swiftly ejected from the congregation. Your former friends are no longer allowed to talk to you and in many cases, your entire social circle will drop you like a hot potato. This practice is known as "Shunning" and can be extremely emotionally painful and scarring for the person being shunned.

My Mum had not been a Witness for very long when this happened so she either didn't know there was a way to return to the religion if you did repent, or perhaps she felt ashamed of being labelled an adulteress and just decided never to look back but either way she had buried it somewhere deep in the recesses of her mind.......until I came along and gave her "That bloody book!" as my Dad now labelled it.

So as though the first bombshell of my Mum having a former religious cult membership wasn't enough I was now being saddled with the worry of what re-joining was going to mean for her? For me? For us as a "family?" and I use that word cautiously as we already felt like a dysfunctional one on so many levels. I now also had the guilt trip laid firmly at my door that if I hadn't brought the book home and raved about it so much she would never have thought about reading it and wanting to re-dedicate her life to God.

It was a turbulent time. Mum had to have more meetings with "The Elders" those stern looking suited men with their extra-large sized bibles. They wanted to meet with her to discuss every intimate detail of her marriages and how she was feeling about everything that had happened in the years since she left.

My Dad at this stage seemed to be very supportive just wanting Mum to be happy and get better and it was probably one of the rare times he actually seemed to give a damn about her. But it was short lived concern because after attending a few meetings where nobody was allowed to speak to Mum until the Elders said they could, Mum was then reinstated and became a member of the local congregation.

This meant big changes! All of a sudden there were rules about everything!

So many rules! Things we weren't allowed to do, say, watch, read, listen to and think!

I was confused.

This lovely book with the pretty animals and everyone getting along that I had loved the message of so much, was now the bane of my life. Along with the rules came the lectures, the fire and brimstone talks over breakfast. The parts I'd either failed to understand or skimmed over in the little burgundy book were all about the fire and sulphur really. In the end, as Mum loved to say, you really only had 2 choices: you were either for God or against him. You couldn't sit on the fence or even sit idle for one single moment! You must pick your side NOW because tomorrow something called Armageddon would come. Once everyone who hadn't picked God had been firebombed from heaven, Jesus was then going to call all the birds down from the sky to his "evening meal" where they would peck everyone's eyes out.

Suddenly the awful news reports and videos of the starving kids didn't seem quite so distressing or urgent, a greater disaster was about to unfold, one that would affect everyone across the globe, not just the children in Africa.

I just wanted to eat my toast and go to school. It's ironic now, looking back, before the whole JW thing I was never fussed on school. Now I just wanted to be on the bus, in class, then on the bus again, anywhere but here, right now, in the kitchen listening to Mum's graphic depictions of the impending doom and destruction.

Somewhere in the midst of this my sister comes to visit, for the first time in many years. Following a bad marriage breakup, she's now a single mother, struggling with postnatal depression and trying her hardest to raise her young daughter. Instead of the lovely family time this should be, Mum leaps at the chance to hone her newfound evangelical skills and having scared me half to death with her Armageddon Alerts, she now lets rip on my sister who sits and takes it, looking terrified. She leaves and I think to myself she's never going to come back now and I don't blame her.

Mum's words have had a profound effect on her though and she soon begins having a bible study, converts and becomes a baptised Jehovah's Witness as well! I figured my sister is pretty sensible so surely she wouldn't become one if it was something really bad, would she? I try to reason it all out in my head as the visions Mum's planted there of sulphur burned bodies and vultures just won't go away.

I say to myself "OK, this God guy sounds really harsh! I'm not entirely sure I want to live in the paradise if I have to see all these horrible things happen, but I suppose I could try to go along with it, if only to make Mum stop ranting about it if nothing else.

There's no way it was ever going to work though. No rock music, or reggae, definitely no heavy metal! No staying up late to watch TV, no boyfriends, or makeup, or masturbating. By now I was a teenager and no teenager ever born wants to have a discussion with their parents about masturbation, never mind have to study a book with several chapters dedicated to the subject, but Jehovah's Witness children - Oh they have to! We were now well into the study of the little blue book, the JW rule book of what young people were allowed to do (not much) and not allowed to do (pretty much everything I wanted to) We were told we weren't allowed to believe in hell as it was a false teaching but that's the best word to describe it.

I'd literally just discovered masturbation and was just beginning to think about boys and booze, now I was being lectured on them morning, noon and night. It was unbearable and I began to feel like I was about to have some kind of mental breakdown myself!

Chapter Six

Horny

Spoiler Alert :

If candid talk about sex is triggering for you, you might want to skip this particular chapter. If on the other hand you are a nosey perv like me, you'll want to hear all of the sordid details so keep right on reading!

For this chapter you will have to forgive me once again for the time hop, but we need to go back in time to several years before the horrible happenings of the previous chapter, to a more innocent time before I was rudely introduced to sex acts in a way I would have preferred never to have seen.

I've forgotten many things over the years but several stick in my mind as though they were yesterday and these are:

The first time I had an orgasm

The first time I saw pornography

The first time I felt really horny and wanted to have sex with a boy,

And the first time I saw a naked man.

Actually, now that I've written them like this I've realised that they happened in exactly this order.

I was very much a tomboy throughout my primary school years and loved nothing better than playing football, climbing trees, riding my bike and skateboarding. My very first orgasm happened whilst climbing a tree funnily enough. I was shinnying up the branches of a large sycamore tree us kids often used to climb because it had an amazing view from the top and it was quite an exhilarating feeling once you were up there, you literally felt on top of the world. On this particular day I was climbing it carefully as I had done many times before and all of a sudden I felt a pulsing feeling between my legs as I was wrapped around the branch. I had no idea what it was and at one point I grabbed so tightly onto the trunk for fear I was going to fall the 20 feet or so to the ground, it was so intense. I'd never experienced anything like it! I remember my ears ringing, my heart thumping in the same rhythm as the pulsing and my vision going all funny, blurry and green tinged. I felt light headed and at one point considered crying out for help as I thought I might not be able to get back down but eventually it subsided and I was left feeling "Wow what the hell was THAT??"

I was only about 9 or 10 at most and naively didn't associate it with sex, partly because I'd had no real form of sex education other than listening to the coarse talk of the farmer's sons in school concerning "shagging". I didn't really know what it was and was too embarrassed to ask. The few brief "birds and bees" lectures I'd had from my Mum mostly consisted of making sure I knew if a man ever came near me I was to scream as loud as I could, if he touched me I was to fight him in any way possible to get away. She nagged me that I shouldn't bite my nails as a woman's greatest weapons were her nails and her voice, for screaming and scratching. This reflects my mum's hatred for violence unless completely necessary because I'm pretty sure if we were having this conversation in the modern day world she would be advising me where the testicles were located and to kick firmly in that area to disable any potential assailant.

Filled with curiosity I decided to seek guidance from the large, very ancient, moth-eaten and dusty book on my parent's bookshelf. It was some kind of prehistoric medical encyclopaedia and of course it contained all kinds of terrifying line drawings of severe abnormalities and ailments of the private parts of both sexes which made me immediately freak out, wonder if there was something terribly wrong with me? and swiftly close it in a cloud of dust.

Shortly after this I was to get some answers albeit not the best source for a young child but everyone has to learn from somewhere I guess. I was playing with some friends and we came across a pile of half burnt magazines in one of their parent's garden. The wife had discovered them, thrown a tantrum and made the husband burn them. Being typical curious kids we fished out all the ones which weren't too charred, took them to our "gang hut" which was an old ramshackle shed and had a laugh looking through the pictures contained within. They were of naked women in various spread eagled poses. Back in those days women had huge hairy muffs and we were all of the age prior to our own pubic hair development so we found the pictures utterly hilarious. One by one everyone was called home for dinner and I was left with the pile of magazines. I picked one up and began reading the stories, I wasn't fussed on looking at the pictures but I wanted to know if the thing I'd experienced was something I was meant to or if it meant there was something "abnormal" going on down there. I started reading and within just a few short paragraphs the pulsating began again. It was a really enjoyable feeling but also at the same time it felt like something I shouldn't really be doing, especially since the hubby of the house had been given a swearing for having them and made to burn them, so in a moment of madness I decided to stuff the magazine inside my jacket and head home to peruse it from the comfort and privacy of my bedroom. I knew if I took the rest of them the others would know so just one seemed like a safe bet.

Once home I could have a proper read. The story, if you could call it that, was something along the lines of a workman who came round to fix a broken washing machine and the woman's fanny got very wet. The man gave her a good licking with his tongue and then fucked her to within an inch of her life. I'd heard the word fuck many times, it was a rural school and kids didn't hold back on using the word even if it wasn't spoken much in our strict household, but I never knew that's what it actually meant. I felt the pulsating 100 times more intensely than the tree incident and now realised......was this what sex was?

I wasn't entirely sure I liked the sound of a man doing that to me, but at the same time I was getting really wet like the woman in the story. Before I knew it I was touching myself inside my pants and there was that amazing fireworks sensation again. I felt like I was dying and being born at the same time. I had to muffle my cries into one of my pillows as I came for the first time actually knowing what it was now and what it was called, for fear someone might hear me. So that was that and I'm not going to lie, my hand was in my pants so much from then on I'm surprised I'm able to see well enough to write this book! Back then people used to say "You'll go blind" if it was a boy playing with himself but they never said what happened to girls or how good any of it actually felt.

Around this time I started looking at boys in a new light and thinking to myself how come I don't want any of them to do that to me?

Wondering if maybe there was something wrong with me because I didn't get wet around the boys my age like the women in the porn mag stories seemed to do, but one night at a local dance there was an older boy and I remember thinking for the first time that I would maybe quite like him to do the things to me that were in the magazine. He wasn't interested in a wee jailbait tomboy like me though, so it was a few more years before I actually experienced any kind of sexual fumbling's or shenanigans with boys. The first couple of boys I got off with I wasn't particularly fussed on and I didn't get wet the way I did at home furtively reading my stories, or making new ones up in my mind. When they tried to push their fingers inside me it just felt painful, dry and awkward. They tried to get me to touch them but I didn't want to reciprocate. One boy started laughing at me and called me a frigid virgin, which to be fair, I was.

One night I was invited to stay at my best friend's house. Her older brother had his best friend over to stay and that brings us to number three on the list which was the first time I really wanted to have sex with a boy. He was funny, good looking and very, very sexy. Finally I'd found a boy who made me wet and I didn't have a broken washing machine, but he was welcome to come round and insert anything he wanted inside me. The only problem was how to be alone with him without my best friend being there, she made it pretty obvious she was feeling the same way. That night as we lay in bed we could hear them carrying on in the room next door, mock fighting and generally being noisy as boys usually are, then he came bursting through the door with just his boxer shorts on and jumped on the bed in-between us. The sexual tension was heavy and thick, you could cut it with a knife. I remember wanting my friend to go so I could touch him, I so badly wanted to run my hands all over his chest and have him kiss me, finger me, ease himself inside me and take my virginity. My parts were pulsating like never before and there was no way to touch myself tonight to relieve it as I was sharing a bed with her. It was sheer hell! I didn't get much sleep that night and I suspect neither did she. All night I fantasised about him doing the things to me from the magazines and decided since he was only staying for a few days if he made a move on me I was totally going to let him go for it. I was painfully shy as a young teen though and I was so awkwardly conscious of the fact every time he came near me I went bright red. I found it hard to talk to him without mumbling and looking away. I couldn't hold his gaze, all I could do was sit there hoping he would read my mind, take the lead and do what was needed to make the aching feeling inside me go away.

A few days later we were all at the local park together and I found myself alone with him, only for a few minutes but he said I was sexy and put his hand on my bum as I walked away. That grope is still etched clearly in my mind as I was throbbing between my legs like never before. I said something lame like I have to be home for my tea, he said he hoped he would see me later. That evening I got a call from my friend, she said the boys wanted to meet up, could I get out for a few hours? Naively I jumped at the chance thinking this would be my opportunity for him to kiss me and things to go further but at the end of the conversation she dropped in that she would be getting off with him and I had to get off with her brother to which I said "no way".

She kept going on and on saying that I had to because otherwise if I didn't go off with him she wouldn't be able to go off with his pal. Really I should just have had a spine and told her to fuck off or made an excuse saying I wasn't allowed out but I was so fanny-led in my decisions, a small voice in my head said well maybe once I've got off with the horrible brother I might get a chance to get off with his pal so it could be worth it? These days you'd call it thirsty or taking one for the team! I was really scraping the barrel as far as self-esteem goes but there you have it. I promised this book would be a warts and all truthful account and as much as I didn't want to go anywhere near her brother, I agreed to meet them in the hope there would be some way I could also have a bit of whatever she was going to be getting.

It didn't work out that way of course, I was landed with the horrible brother in the gang hut, I remember him roughly grabbing my hand, pushing it down his unzipped jeans and showing me how to give him a wank. I shut my eyes, thought about his good looking friend and tossed him off as quickly as I could so there might be a chance I could do the same to him too. That never happened and it ended up that my friend took great pleasure in telling me the following day in intimate details all the great sexy things they did and how good it was. How she was sorry she could tell I liked him, but he couldn't go with me and leave her and her brother sitting together like gooseberries. She wasn't sorry of course, this was just yet another in a long string of things she seemed to deliberately do to hurt me or emotionally control me. This was the first of many times I settled for less than I deserved though and didn't stand up for myself. The good news though was I now knew that there were boys who made me want to have sex even if it was only this one I couldn't have, it gave me hope one day I would find a different one I felt the same way about and it would all click into place.

Seeing a naked man came a couple of years later, I was walking the dog and happened to glance across at one of the neighbour's cottages as the light was on, the curtains were open and it was dark so I could see him but he couldn't see me. I was mesmerised, he was just standing naked without a care in the world, changing the channel on the TV and strolling around his living room. I didn't get any funny feelings down below but I did have a giggle as I walked home. I was pressured to tell Mum as she wanted to know why I took so long to come home. I stupidly thought she might find it amusing too, but she didn't, she went mental and told my Dad, who also went mental. I was shouted and bawled at as though I had done something sinful by looking when I should have averted my eyes, then I was shouted at some more and told never to walk the dog past his house ever again. Then my Dad got really angry and said he was going to go round and beat him up for being a flasher and a pervert.

Oh how I really regretted telling Mum. I felt genuinely sorry for the man he wasn't doing anything wrong he was probably just enjoying a moment of nakedness after coming out of the shower as you do, although I prefer to close my curtains but hey each to their own! I begged with my Dad to please not cause a scene. I hated his guts as it was and it pained me to even be having a conversation with him full stop, but I didn't think it was right this man should take a beating just because he was jealous. I realise now that that's exactly what he was because after this incident, he decided well, I had seen the neighbour naked so he might as well parade around the house in the buff. So began the awful spectacle of my Dad constantly being either completely nude or in his horrible grotty underpants. It was insufferable, I used to try to look at anything except him and get out of his way as quickly as possible which wasn't always easy as he would often stand in the narrow hallway before the toilet so if you were really needing to go you had to pass him.

On several occasions when I was in my room and I knew he was downstairs naked, I'd have to pee into the saucer underneath the plant pot in my room and then throw it out of the window. I figured doing that was better than having to try to press myself flat against the wall of the corridor to get past him to use the actual toilet. Horrible, perverted bastard that he was. It's only now as an adult I piece together what was really happening, he had decided in his mind that I was now "ripe and ready" or come of age for sexual abuse. Except he had one big problem and that was that I hated him with a passion and would have screamed absolute blue murder if he so much as went near me. I would barricade myself in my room rather than be anywhere near him alone so his naked parading only served to make me more determined than ever to make sure he never got an opportunity to.

Chapter 7

Hallucinating

Unsurprisingly, not long after the Horrible Happenings, my parents' marriage really went tits up. There was a brief period, urged on by the Elders to try to make her marriage work like a good Christian wifey, Mum would do this really fake giggle, hang on my Dad's every word, cook him huge lavish breakfasts and basically bend over backwards in every way apart from the main way he wanted her to, to try and salvage what remained of their shambolic relationship. This absolutely infuriated me to say the least. I was already a very angry, angst ridden young woman filled with raging hormones and temper tantrums as, rightly so, I believed my Father was now "outed" as a sexual pervert and paedophile and shouldn't have even been still living in the house, but what the Elders said was what Mum went by even when he started cheating on her left, right and centre and turning up the heat on the sexual pressure he was putting her under.

These were turbulent times. I hated him before, but now I was determined to do everything in my power to sabotage him even if it was only in small ways. I began stealing his money, cigarettes and booze from the drinks cabinet, replacing the spirits with water. It's odd the way we become the things we loathe, I was not a fan of drinking or smoking, knowing both of them to be unhealthy but I was lashing out in the only way I knew how. Mum was constantly trying to lecture me about not drinking, not smoking, not going near boys and not ever under any circumstances going near drugs but all I heard was blah, blah, blah. My teenage rebellion was in full sway. She thought I might be likely to do these things because of peer group pressure but the truth was I wanted to do them because I wanted to cause as much hell for him as possible so he might leave.

I also wanted to numb the dirty feelings I had inside any time I flashed back to what had happened. Alcohol provided a means of escape into oblivion even if only for a short time. Plus I lost all respect for Mum the minute she let him just get away with what he did and then lowered herself by trying everything she could to make him happy. I felt so many emotions whirling around inside me. Anger, disgust, shameful dirtiness, fear of what was going to happen to me if all the things Mum said about Armageddon were true, heavily laced with an urgency to try to do everything I could in my power to get him to leave or if that didn't work I decided I would leave instead.

At one point I packed my school bag with some clothes and possessions and tried to think where would be the best place to go, but when it came down to it, I didn't want to desert Mum as I knew he would make life even more unbearable for her if I wasn't there. So I stayed and tried to do everything I could to make her see sense. One evening she was emptying his pockets ready for the wash and as she put the loose change on the table a condom wrapper fell out. She either didn't notice or pretended not to. I made sure she saw it though and as much as it hurt me to see her upset I knew she needed to open her eyes to what was going on. Dad had a vasectomy after I was born so there was only one reason it was there!

Shortly after, I came home from school one day and found her crying. He had been trying to sexually assault her but luckily she managed to escape and barricaded herself in her room. An argument ensued where he blamed her for their marriage going wrong because she was no longer giving him oral or anal sex. Jehovah's Witnesses frown very heavily on these things you see, back then there were strict policies on everything married couples were allowed to do, or not do in the bedroom. Whilst on one hand the stern men in suits were lecturing her about trying to be a more compliant wife as divorce is frowned upon, they were also telling her she must only stick to vanilla, common garden variety sex. So my poor Mum was being badgered by my Dad constantly. This breaking point led to him admitting to numerous affairs. Mum now had the option to separate and divorce him as Jehovah's Witnesses are only allowed to "scripturally divorce" if adultery is proven or admitted. Mum now had both and I begged her again and again to get shot of him once and for all and she finally agreed.

Things had really come to a head for me too, I was constantly filled with all these awful feelings and having no coping mechanism for them I was resorting to binge drinking whenever I got the chance, spending as much time out of the house as I possibly could even if it was just walking the dog in the rain or hanging around the local park on my own in the cold, anything was better than being at home listening to them arguing, slamming doors, my Dad punching holes in the doors and Mum crying once he left.

Things got so bad that even school which had become a means of getting away from it all was no longer a refuge. I was plagued with feelings of self-loathing, hatred, worthlessness and dirtiness. It didn't help that my friends were all beginning to experiment with different styles and makeup. I wasn't allowed to wear any due to Mum's strict beliefs, it was such a battle to get her to see my point of view on anything. Everything had to be checked with the Bible to make sure it was OK. Even though women adorning themselves with jewellery or braiding their hair existed thousands of years ago, Mum felt this was relevant source material to make sure I wasn't going to commit a sin in the modern world.

I wasn't the best looking teenager, I was gawky and awkward with bright red cheeks and no eyebrows, I was an odd shape too, skinny with no boobs or curves anywhere. All my friends were developing lumps and bumps in all the right places, some of them had love bites and not just on their necks. They wore them as a badge of pride to show they had a boyfriend or at the very least, had a good time at the weekend. Then there was me - the ugly duckling amongst all the swans. I felt so awkward as I was mesmerised by looking at what everyone else had and I didn't, one girl in particular kept catching my roving eye. She was everything I wanted to be but wasn't. She was kind, funny, quirky, confident, interesting and busty as hell. I felt oddly drawn to her and started to wonder if I was a lesbian? I liked boys more though so was I bi? I decided to shelve these thoughts and feelings and just try to focus on getting through each day without adding any extra baggage to the quagmire of shit I was trying to wade through on a daily basis.

Eventually I managed to persuade Mum to let me buy some red reducing foundation for my cheeks and have my hair permed and ears pierced so I could at least have some semblance of being a normal teenager. She reluctantly agreed and everyone said what a difference this transformation made. I was now starting to look more like a girl, I started to get boys taking more of an interest in me, although never the ones I really liked, but at least I was beginning to blend in a little on the outside even if inside I was a fucked up mess.

One day it all just overwhelmed me and I could feel myself about to start crying for no reason, it was all just too much I couldn't keep all of it inside any longer. I told the teacher I wasn't feeling well and was sent to the sick bay. I laid on the bed wishing I could just stay there forever and not have to go home. Sick bay was a truly gruesome place with posters about nits and other parasitic organisms plastered around the walls, so this lets you know how bad it was that I preferred to be there than with my classmates. After what seemed like ages a very nice male teacher came in and asked me what was wrong, on the verge of tears I managed to summon up the courage to tell him that things were really bad at home and I didn't want to ever go back there please could he help me?

He left and a short while later my parents arrived to take me home. I couldn't believe it! Any chance I had of ever being able to trust anyone or tell them what was really going on was now completely blown out of the water. I felt like everyone was against me, everything was hopeless and I couldn't see a way out, it felt like a thick fog I was battling through every day just to try to make sense of the world around me. My so called best friend at the time, the one who got off with the guy I liked wasn't much of a help either. She was really a manipulative, narcissistic bully who loved nothing better than to make my already gloomy outlook even more depressing. Her favourite mind game was to tell me things people had apparently said about me, always bad of course never anything nice. She seemed to take a sick, twisted pleasure in telling me things to upset me, watching my reaction then saying "I just thought you should know. I mean I would want to know if it were me"

The final straw came one day I'd just had enough of her, she was trying to tell me something horrible a neighbour had said about me and I just lost it and told her to fuck off. I knew the neighbour hadn't said anything of the kind she was a lovely elderly woman who would never say a bad word against anyone. My so called friend wasn't used to verbal kickbacks, she was a spoiled brat who always got what she wanted, one way or another. She decided to teach me a lesson, as punishment for my rebellion against her controlling behaviour, she would get her older brother, the horrible one I had wanked off, to tell everyone about it and make me sorry for saying that. I didn't care and told her to fuck off and do whatever she wanted to do. I was past the point of caring and it felt really good to finally stand up to her after months of her mental torture on top of everything else I was already dealing with. I was soon to regret it though!

The big brother started on me immediately, on the school bus home, kicking and shoving the back of my seat and calling me names getting everyone else to join in and laugh at me. The next day the whole school knew what I had done and I started getting people laughing at me, making jibes, calling me names. I didn't think I was a slut for what I had done, it felt more like something I'd been emotionally blackmailed into doing. Somehow though, everyone in the school was now looking at me differently, like I was dirty and soiled. The seat kicking and name calling carried on the next day and the next, I knew I would have to get back in her "good books" again for it to stop. I held my tears and anger in until I got home and then ran to my room and just sobbed my heart out. Why was my life so shite? Why was everything in it going wrong? Was it ever going to get any better? Mum's answer of course was "Pray to Jehovah" the bog standard JW reply to any problem life might throw at you. Just pray to him and he'll fix everything! Except of course if you have hatred in your heart and you drink, smoke, masturbate and want to have sex with boys, and possibly girls too? Then you can't pray to him because you're too dirty and sinful to approach him. When Armageddon comes you can bet your boots there's going to be some very large carrion birds sitting in the trees outside your house, just waiting to peck your eyes out as you expire. So I just lie on my bed sobbing and hoping the dark, black blanket of sleep will make it all go away even just for a short while.

Somewhere in the middle of all this, I meet a boy. Two of my friends have been on a caravan holiday and met three boys, they hook up with one each which leaves one spare. They ring me nagging me to come meet him. He's really nice, he really wants to meet me and I need to come over, it'll be loads of fun. Back in those days getting permission to do anything was like pulling teeth but somehow I managed to convince Mum I was going to meet my friends for a couple of hours, nothing untoward was going to happen and I'd be back in time for tea. The minute I clapped eyes on him he gave me the "ick" he was very tall, gangly, awkward and had a strange walk, not to mention the fact he had ginger curly hair and weird eyes. I told my friends straight I wasn't interested but they kept going on and on, I should give him a chance and then the words I'll never forget - that I had never had a boyfriend and what the hell was wrong with me? He had a car and was older, what was I thinking saying No?

The not so subtle message played right into my deep rooted self-esteem issues. I was an ugly virgin, this was about as good an offer as I was ever going to get, so I went off for a drive with him just to get them to shut up and stop teasing me. He was actually an OK guy and I found I was able to fantasise about him being lots of other boys if I shut my eyes and concentrated really hard when he was kissing me or feeling me up. After a while it wasn't all bad as he seemed really smitten with me. He was always writing me poems, making me mix tapes (the ultimate declaration of love in the 80's) buying me gifts and telling me how much he liked me. He was so not my type though.

One night at a party all my friends were laughing and teasing me. One boy shouted across the gap between records that his hairstyle made him look like he had a dead cat on his head. I was mortified, I didn't want to be seen with him so I ignored him for most of the night, which upset him. We managed to get past it though and the times we did spend together in his car or at his house were my chance to escape my horrible home life, even if it was just for a short while. I was able to conjure up mental images of the tall, dark, handsome boys I fancied who of course never fancied me back, and imagine it was them I was with instead. This went on for a few months until I turned 16, looking back it was a bit pervy really as he was in his 20s and I was a 15 year old virgin, but on the night of my 16th birthday, we had agreed to wait until then, we had sex in his bedroom.

It was awful! I remember a searing hot pain, much disappointment and instant regret. I wanted to go home which was unheard of, going home was always my least favourite part of spending time with him, but I knew I couldn't go through that again, was this really what all the fuss was about? I felt really disillusioned and ended things the next day. He was gutted of course and wrote me letters and called me, trying in vain to get me to give him another chance but my mind was made up. I wasn't doing any of that stuff again unless it was with someone I actually fancied and because I wanted to.

I suppose I have to concede that my Dad was the only reason I was even allowed to have a boyfriend as Mum was completely against the idea. She was torn between abhorring the idea of me, her youngest daughter being a "fornicator" and having to obey the headship rule where my Dad had the final say. She took every possible opportunity to lecture me on AIDS which at that time was an emerging world crisis. As well as putting myself at physical risk, I was also risking my eternal life in the paradise because Jehovah doesn't want people who enjoy sinning. As she was fond of reminding me, if you commit a sexual sin you're doing it against your own body as well as God. It seemed whatever I did, whichever direction I turned in I was doing something wrong. I was sick of being dragged to the Kingdom Hall and teased at school for having a crazy hippy and a "Jehovah's Biscuit" for a Mother. I figured well I might as well just go for it then if I'm going to die in the fireball fest I may as well try to have some fun in the process.

I'm not entirely sure why my Dad was happy to let this play out, usually normal Dad's want to deter young men from violating their daughters. Perhaps because he thought it might make it easier for him to grab an opportunity to have me himself? Let some young stud groom me so he didn't have to? He had now progressed to new levels of creepiness, making lewd comments about my female classmates to the point I wasn't able to have friends come and stay at my house like a normal teenager, and standing outside my bedroom door late at night, I would hear him climb the stairs and pause on the landing outside my door, he would be heavy breathing, I'd lie there heart pounding ready to scream the place down if he ever came in. Thankfully he never did, maybe he was just happy to get me out of the house so he could torment Mum without my prying eyes, I'll probably never know but I'm just glad I managed to escape when I did.

One day I come home from school and Mum tells me she's getting a divorce and moving out. She's been busy behind the scenes and all the

JW's who thought she should try harder to please my Dad now agree it's toxic, she needs to get away from him as fast as possible. They have pulled together to organise a caravan for her to live in next door to a JW family. I can come and live with her and it'll all be great. This is the best news I've heard in a long time, but my elation doesn't last long as Mum starts telling me all the rules involved. I must be a good JW daughter as she will be a single parent so will have full responsibility over me. I'll be 16 and legally an adult but we follow God's laws not those of mere men. I can't have posters on my wall or listen to rock music or stay out late and I must attend 3 meetings a week at the Kingdom Hall, a place I'm already beginning to loathe with a passion. Don't get me wrong, everyone there's so super nice you can feel the sugar dripping off their tongues, everyone wants to hug each other and compliment everyone else, surely nobody can be that nice in real life is it just an act they put on in public?

I remember the stern Elders who didn't seem so nice and helpful and I don't think the 2 images correlate very well. It's normal to have doubts Mum tells me but I must brush them to one side, I must behave myself, keep studying the blue book telling me not to masturbate, which is about as much use as a chocolate fireguard, because masturbating is one of my favourite hobbies right now. As the scripture she's oft fond of quoting says, I must pummel my body and lead it as a slave. I laugh inwardly to myself if she only knew the ways I was actually pummelling it! My heart sinks though. I genuinely don't know what to do. I go to school the following day and my friends sense something is wrong. Suzie the girl who gives me those weird mixed up feelings wants to know what's up am I OK? In a rare moment of clarity and bravery I tell her I'm going to be homeless and she says she thinks she can help! A woman her sister babysits for has a room going for rent, perhaps I could move in there?

It's an absolute God send and I'm so grateful to her. Mum reluctantly agrees, my Dad is left to foot the bill as I pack my belongings, racing to my newfound freedom as fast as my legs will carry me!

As great as it is to finally be free, without any form of parental restriction I now begin a speedy descent into debauchery. I don't get a large allowance each week but every penny

goes on fags, booze, entry into young farmer's
discos and dances and all I want to do is get
drunk, have a laugh with my friends and get it
on with boys. The more sensible of my friends
actually try to talk some sense into me at times,
they're worried I'm going off the rails, that I'm
going to mess up my education and career
prospects and that I'm getting a reputation,
which of course are all true and deep down I
know they're right, but I shrug it all off and just
keep partying and making mistakes. I'm damn
well sampling everything I think I've been
missing out on and that brings us to the night
me and a friend decide to drop some acid.
Everyone else is doing it so we decide to give it
a try.

At first it seems like a fun idea, we'll go to stay
at a friend's house and just have a laugh and
see where the night takes us. When we get there
though, her elderly mum is very grumpy and
orders us upstairs to bed and to be quiet. When
we get to her room she gets into bed and me
and my friend look at each other and realise
were coming up. We get the giggles and start
talking the biggest load of shite ever. We stare
at our faces in the mirror and watch them
shape-shift, it's funny and slightly scary and

then funny again. Trying-to-get-to-sleep friend keeps telling us to shut the fuck up and downstairs her grumpy ma' shouts up similar expletives and that we'd better not be doing drugs up there!

My tripping friend is freaking out a bit now as she's convinced her hands are turning into a bunch of bananas, I manage to reassure her that they're not whilst stifling almost uncontrollable waves of giggles. I decide to go to the loo to gather my thoughts. I'm sitting on the toilet for what seems like forever just enjoying the sensations and I become aware gradually that there's a radio playing away quietly in the background, I think to myself we better turn that off or our friend's Mum will go mental, we don't want her coming upstairs and seeing us like this. I think I'd quite like a nice tall, cold glass of water and after what seems like an age suddenly there is one sitting there beside me! I don't remember anyone coming in, or filling it myself, how did it get there? I then realise I've been sitting on the toilet this whole time with my clothes on. Did I do the toilet? I don't remember going? I don't even know if I need to go. This is weird. Maybe I should drink

the water then I'll feel like going. I go to drink
the glass of water and it's empty.

I'm freaking out a wee bit now so I go in to see
if my friend's OK and if her hands have turned
back into hands again. She's staring at them but
not freaking out as much and she says they're
becoming smaller bananas now. In a vain
attempt to focus on something I pick up a
magazine and say "Let's do the crossword" we
then have hilarious fun for what seems like
hours we get all of the answers correct and
every single one elicits streams of laughter. The
radio is still playing but it doesn't seem so loud
now so I just enjoy the background music it's
providing. My friend then says she's tired so let's
go to sleep. Great idea except I'm not the
slightest bit tired, I'm wired to the moon and
buzzing off my tits. My poor sober friend says
"Yeah please just go to sleep youse are doing
my head in your never staying here again!" so I
reluctantly climb into bed. I lie there listening to
the music which is now becoming loud and
annoying so I ask my tripping friend if she can
turn it off as it sounds like she's closer. She
grunts that there isn't a radio playing. I don't
believe her as a short while ago she thought her
hands were bananas so I ask my sober friend

where is it so I can turn it off myself. She gets really angry and tells me we are a pair of bampots. There isn't a radio and hasn't been one playing all night. This really freaks me out as I'm left with the realisation that the music is playing inside my head. I lie there in the dark feeling really weird, scared, alone, wanting it all to just STOP. I try to control the music and fail, eventually I just lie there powerless, listening to it along with the sound of both my friends snoring until the dawn breaks and it's time to go home. I haven't had a wink of sleep and feel really odd! I don't like it and am looking forward to it wearing off so I can finally go home to bed. I pick up the magazine before I leave and the words in the boxes make no sense at all, not a single one of them is a correct answer and some of the letters look back to front. I decide there and then I am never ever dropping acid again as long as I live because this was not fun at all and I think that's the end of it, but really it's just the beginning of a new and even more fucked up chapter.

Chapter 8

Homeless

After the Acid trip night things become one big, drunken, messed up blur. I feel weird all the time, disjointed, ill at ease in my own body - it's become this strange entity I'm not in control of the way I was before. I keep having odd moments where I feel weird sensations and feel panicky for no apparent reason. I don't know they are flashbacks as there was no Google back then to look things up, so I just try to go deeper down the only hole I know to escape it all. I'm failing at every subject at school except English, my teachers are nagging me that I need this and that to go to Uni. All my friends are going to college or Uni but I can barely face getting up and dressed in the morning.

All I want to do when I come home from School is watch films and drink, smoke, party and snog boys. I've still not found a boy yet that I want to try sex with again to see if it all clicks into place and works better with someone you fancy, but it doesn't take me long to find one. My lodgings are directly next to a pub and one night a drunken guy knocks on the door, he's looking for my friend Suzie's sister who babysits sometimes. I tell him she's not here and look him up and down, he looks me up and down and I think "Hmmm, not bad". Tall, dark, handsome, big sideburns. These were the basic requirements for me back then. Probably still are, if I'm honest!

He asks if he can come in and I agree but we have to keep very quiet, my landlady will go mad if I break the no boys rule, even though she has a guy she sneaks in the back door when her kids are in bed. I catch her one night and she asks me through gritted teeth to keep it to myself. That's my leverage to throw the no boys rule right out of the downstairs window I begin to sneak him in through any chance I get. We start seeing each other and do pretty much everything but go the whole way. I'm actually starting to quite like him and feel ready to, when he announces he's going off on a lad's holiday. They have a competition every year to see who can get off with the most girls. I've not to worry though because it's just harmless holiday fun, it doesn't mean anything and it's me he really loves.

I may have been through a hard time and done some messed up stuff but this doesn't sound like a good deal to me so I tell him it's over, he's to enjoy his holiday and I up and leave. Men are just such a disappointment so I decide right there the next one I meet I will just use him purely as a sexual object and not bother to form any sort of relationship or feelings.

I don't have to wait very long, there's a dance on and a guy who's much too old for me, I have my beady eye on him. I've already been warned by my landlady I've not to go near him if I do there will be consequences. He's a workmate of the guy I've just broken up with and my landlady's ever increasing attempts to try to bring in parental replacement are really starting to piss me off, so I decide this is a great way to kill two birds with one stone. I gulp down the usual cheap rocket fuel cider and Thunderbird and head to the dance. I make a beeline for the guy, we go home together and he fucks me hard in his purple bedroom. We're both very drunk but it feels good, he's well endowed, it's exciting and I'm feeling devilishly rebellious. I'm also relieved that my second time around was enjoyable and there are no strings attached. It's a small town though and word gets around. My ex comes back from holiday, he's banging on the door drunk saying he loves me and please will I take him back? A sensible friend says I should give him a chance but I refuse. The other guy comes to the door and I end up telling him to bugger off as well. Landlady is now furious that I've somehow managed to show her up by sleeping with him, am I not ashamed of myself? No, I'm not and she can bugger off as well and just like that I'm homeless again.

Luckily, sober friend's older sister takes me in and I stay with her for a short time while I'm awaiting my work placement in London. Having thoroughly messed up my education prospects I decide to drop out of school so I can really make a balls up of my life by drinking, smoking and partying more than ever before in the short wait before my 6 month work experience job in London begins. With little prospects or guidance in anything, a teacher suggests this option to me and it seems like an exciting opportunity, perhaps a chance to have a fresh start from everyone and everything that's making me so desperately unhappy.

Because when the hangover kicks in and I wake up with a different boy in my bed - there's been a string of them now, I just feel empty, dirty and annoyed with myself. I don't much like this path

I'm on, it feels like the "broad and spacious road leading off into destruction" that Mum was always banging on about. I've tried the alternative path though and it's just too restrictive, I don't seem able to do anything in moderation right now. The radio that played the night of the acid trip has now steadily evolved into two distinct voices instead of background music. I name them Angel and Devil, they reside on my opposite shoulders. Angel is female, she tries to get me to see sense. "Listen to your sensible friends, they know you best, go back to school, eat humble pie, make amends with your Mum. Stop partying so hard, stop shagging all these boys, don't smoke! it's bad for you, you need help!

You're going to die at Armageddon if you don't stop!"

Devil is male, he's like that boy always trying it on, daring you to do stuff, He says "Your only young once enjoy it to the max! Fuck everyone who tries to tell you otherwise or stop you". They battle away with their opposing opinions and I'm powerless to control them other than drowning them out with booze or the addictive buzz of getting off with someone new for the first time.

Somewhere in the midst of a very drunken night I end up brawling with my friend and knocking her teeth out. I don't remember where, why or anything. All of a sudden she's standing over me yelling, covered in blood and I don't have a clue how it happened.

Another night I'm sitting on the stairs to our flat and she's shouting in my face because she's fed up with my behaviour and wants me gone. I attempt to tell her what happened with my Dad and all the demons that are tormenting me ever since but I either don't find the right words, or what I do say is so repulsive to her she belts me one right across the face. Not enough to knock any of my teeth out but it's definitely a revenge hit.

I've outstayed my welcome once again.

I'm not really caring though as trying to tell her was a last ditch attempt. Whether knowingly, or unknowingly, I was pressing the self-destruct button with all my might. There was a trail of devastation I was blazing wherever I went, burning bridge after bridge. My paltry effort is too little too late, I'm soon packing my bags to leave for London, or should I say bag because each time I get kicked out of each successive place on my downward spiral, I leave behind or give away belongings so I can travel light. I head south to what I hope will be a fresh start. It's make or break time!

Arriving in London I immediately feel out of my depth. I've only ever lived in small villages and towns in the countryside. Suddenly I'm on the outskirts of the capital city and surrounded by people of colour. I feel so silly writing this now as an adult, but back then I'd only previously seen coloured people on TV, never in real life. Now I look around anxiously to find other white people and there are none. There's also the fact that I lied on my job application saying I can cook. I'm here to look after a bed bound disabled man and I can barely boil an egg. Luckily I come clean and the lovely man that he is, he's happy to keep this quiet and teach me how to cook in return for me giving him a small alcoholic drink with his night time medication. Something he's not really supposed to have according to the big, burly nurses who come in several times a week and shout at me for doing everything wrong, as well as the previous carer who's a really churchy, goody goody type who stays for a few days to make sure I'm not going to fuck everything up and undo all her good work.

Somehow I manage to blunder through the next few months, my wee man is so nice and patient. He calls out instructions to me from his bed as I slave over the stove in the kitchen and with his help, I learn to cook a few basic dishes which we enjoy together over a shared love of music. He tells me stories of times he played in bands, women he loved, stars he met and jammed with like Jimi Hendrix.

I don't want to leave the flat, it feels safe and I feel a sense of purpose, but I have to go out to do shopping for fresh ingredients which terrifies me. I seem to be developing into this anxious, paranoid, nervous wreck with a hefty dose of agoraphobia and insomnia thrown in for good measure. When I've finished my chores each day, I find myself a whirling mess of anxieties and worries, as though the trip I took so recently has opened some kind of dark wormhole in the recesses of my mind. Out of which every kind of insecurity and negative thought can just appear and consume me. I lie on my bed and try to read, the page blurs, the words jump around on the page and merge together, there are flashes of light, my heart pounds. Everything outside is so noisy, there's no woods or tranquil fields to escape to, just a concrete jungle filled with dark underpasses I must walk through with my racing heart convinced I will be murdered. Foreign sounding and smelling shops I must navigate to get the food we need to make the dishes he likes best and worst of all I feel so desperately lonely for the first time in my life. I'm pretending to be this independent, adventurous young woman, but really I feel like a scared little kid.

I look at myself in the mirror and I get flashbacks to the mirror in my friend's room when we were tripping. The lights go strange colours and my face looks weird. Every tiny blemish suddenly seems huge, my pupils look like big black saucers, my skin so pale, my breathing shallow. I'm the whitest, palest person in a 10 mile radius. I still have a photo from this time period and when I look at it now I think if only I could see how pretty I was back then and slim, no double chin or chubby cheeks. My complexion was great and I was so youthful looking but I was thin because I was burning off so much nervous energy. I look unhappy because I'm stressed all the time and feeling homesick, missing my friends and my boyfriend.

He writes me love letters saying how much he misses me but it's not enough. I'm not sure I can cope. I buy some red hair dye and change my hair in a desperate attempt to have something interesting and distracting to look at when I see myself. I dabble with different makeup styles and eventually come to the realisation that no matter what I do, this is not going to work. I've aimed too high with no support net underneath me and now I'm in freefall. I've made a monumental mess of things, I need to eat humble pie, admit I'm falling apart at the seams and return home.

One thing I miss most of all is the company of my pet dog. This is the longest I've ever been without canine company and it feels awful not to have a doggy pal to cuddle and tell all my troubles to or feel safer when I venture out for walks.

Once again, I pack my ever smaller growing bag of possessions and head home to Scotland to find my boyfriend has been cheating on me, my friend I'm supposed to be getting a flat with has met the love of her life and I've nowhere to live once again. Luckily her Mother agrees to take me in until I can get sorted. I feel like such a failure at everything, a real "down and out" I get a job in a boarding kennels which does make me happy because I'm back spending time with dogs again, but I'm drinking too much, not eating enough and constantly caught in this terrible cycle of feeling like something awful is happening or about to happen to me. At times it feels like the sky is going to come crashing in on top of me. I'm almost afraid to look up at it, the dizziness is overwhelming. Sometimes it's so hard to breathe. I don't know what anxiety is yet at this point, so I've no idea how to articulate it or who I would even begin to tell.

One day at work it all gets too much and I have to sit down for a few minutes. My head is spinning and I feel like I'm going to faint? die? I'm not sure what? My boss comes to ask me what's wrong. I'm cautious with my words as she seems to have it in for me. I have to walk about a mile to catch the last bus home and several times now she's kept me working late so I miss it. I think to myself she must know if I miss it I'll have to walk home does she literally not care? Sometimes I'm able to hitchhike home which in itself is pretty scary. Angel voice likes telling me I'll be picked up by a psycho and murdered, Devil says just get home, you've got a cold bottle waiting in the fridge for you, once you down that everything will be ok again. A few times I have to walk the 5 or 6 miles after already walking dogs and cleaning kennels all day. I sense my jackets on a slack nail so I tell her I'm not feeling well and that I feel really worried. She sends me home and then decides to sack me as one of the lovely other girls who works there tells her I drink and take drugs. Thanks!

So, I'm jobless again, living on the good charity of my friend's Mum who really could be doing without the hassle. Her teenage daughter has barely flown the nest, now she's stuck with a far worse one she hardly knows, who's on the verge of a nervous breakdown.

Everything comes to a head and she suggests I go to the Doctors, I'm not eating properly or sleeping and I'm just a walking bag of nerves anytime I'm not sober. The Doctor listens briefly to my story, scribbles in the notes that I am an alcoholic and prescribes me a potent cocktail of anti-psychotic drugs and sleeping pills which make me absolutely one million percent worse. At one point I'm lying on my friend's bed wishing I was dead because there's voices in my head that the pills are meant to stop, but instead they're getting louder, more insistent and impossible to tune out or control. My body which felt odd before, now feels completely alien to me. I'm twitching and convulsing and panicking. I don't know if I'm going to die and part of me wants to because living sucks so badly right now.

Bill and Ted from the posters on my friend's bedroom wall laugh at me, talk to me, goad me to take an overdose. I just want to fall into a deep, restful sleep and never wake up. The sound of my heartbeat becomes unbearable - it's like a ticking time bomb.

"Boom.....boom......boom" goes my chest, the erratic beat travelling right up into my throat, so forcefully my hands shake in a symbiotic rhythm. I gave up on praying a long time ago, but if I did, I'd ask God to please send me someone to help me, to make it all go away. I meet a boy and he's not really my type but he has a motorbike and a leather jacket. When I'm with him the voices are a bit quieter, I can block them out, relax a tiny bit and have a few laughs so I agree to go out with him.

Suddenly one day the people from the Council and the Barnardo's charity come and offer me a house. I jump for joy! Hopefully this will be my fresh start this time where things start to look up. A place I can call my own, I'll be able to have my own dog again, I've missed having one so much!

Chapter 9

Huntin' Hounds

Spoiler Alert :

It would be really easy for me to pander to the "snowflake generation" of today and omit this chapter from my memoir, but when I began writing this book I promised myself it would be a true and honest account of my life experiences to date. Hunting with, and shooting over dogs was such a huge part of my life for 30 years it seems wholly wrong to just pretend this part never happened.

However, I respect that this may be extremely upsetting for some people, so I advise you to skip to the next chapter if you think it will be triggering for you.

"Sick Bitch"

"Psycho"

"You're a wrong 'un"

"Your evil"

Every name you can think of I've been called it, but when people find out you enjoy fieldsports, this always brings out the most vitriolic of insults.

The fact of the matter is, I always loved dogs more than people and preferred their company. If I'd had a more stable childhood I might never have discovered and become addicted to hunting with them, but a bad homelife coupled with a constant desire to escape and be out in nature meant I discovered this unusual path. Never being one to go with convention, these hobbies became a constant feature throughout most of my adult life.

In primary school I was always doodling cartoon dogs and my teacher who was a dog breeder herself noticed this and fed my ever growing desire to learn, by giving me her old books and magazines. A particular favourite was the one about dog breeding. I don't imagine there are many ten year olds who decide they want to be a dog breeder and study genetics in their spare time, but my teacher had started a fire that couldn't be put out. I knew there and then that was what I wanted to do,

much to the disgust and odd looks from
everyone I told about my future vocation.

The first time I saw a lurcher was in a black and
white photo in a book on a school trip. I was a
bookworm from an early age and encouraged
by Mum who was happy I enjoyed reading as
much as she did. I would pore over any books I
could get my hands on from the library. I'd buy
any I could get with my pocket money,
especially so on school trips and special
occasions, non-fiction was my favourite. If I
found a subject I was interested in then I
wanted to know everything there was to know
about it.

My previous obsession was a book about seaside
plants, animals and birds. We never visited the
seaside much, living so far inland, so on the rare
occasions we did, I would just breathe in the sea
air, close my eyes and listen to the birds calling
and waves washing against the shore. I'd collect
shells and unusual stones like treasures and try
to save these memories, transporting myself
back into them whilst reading the book in my
bedroom back home. I've always wanted to live
near the beach ever since this first trip, perhaps
one day I'll be able to make it a reality. The

quaint little white cottage with the wooden gate leading to the shore I pictured in my mind's eye as a child.

Back to the dogs though. If I remember rightly the book was a small pamphlet type called "Old Working Dogs" or something similar and the photo was of a bearded, smock clad warrener sitting atop a dug out warren with his cream rough coated lurcher, having his lunch.

Something about this photo struck a chord deep inside me. Minus the beard, I could almost instantly visualise myself sitting in this same scenario enjoying nature and happily eating my lunch outside in the sun. Funnily enough the family of dogs I owned for all the years I hunted are almost identical to the dog from this iconic photo. I made it my mission to learn all about lurchers! Information was scant but I was able to deduce they were a mixture of various sighthound and non-sighthound breeds such as collie cross greyhound or Bedlington terrier cross whippet and I became fascinated with the idea of owning one.

I hated my Dad but he held the key. I would sneak into his office when he was at work, find his Exchange and Mart magazines and circle in pen all the adverts for lurchers I liked the sound of.

"HJKC" meant hunt, jump, kill and carry. This was the main requirement for the dog to be considered useful at its job.

"Untried" usually meant the dog had been tried out and found wanting in some way.

The adverts were mesmerising to me, so many secret code words to decipher. It was as though the people who owned them had their own mystical language.

They were very cheap too! You could pick one up for between £20 and £30 and I had more money than that saved up from my pocket money. I was saving for a pair of bell bottom flare jeans, one of the few fashions Mum deemed acceptable since she also wore them, but I wanted a lurcher more. A lurcher meant excitement, freedom and illicit forays into the countryside.

Eventually my parents asked me if I would like a dog of my own as I'd walked the legs off our family pet dog. She was becoming grumpy and geriatric and my Dad's security guard dog he took to work wasn't suitable as a pet. I was so excited at the prospect but as always my parents had to thwart my cunning plans.

"You're not getting one of those gypsy dogs"

"They need too much exercise"

My arguments about having the money to pay for it and exercise it myself fell on deaf ears and it was decided a Labrador would be a much wiser investment as a family pet. I never understood this as it was more expensive, they had to buy the puppy for me and we had to travel much further to get the puppy, but any puppy was better than none. I resolved secretly to use it to hunt the way a lurcher would, when it was old enough, so it would be a makeshift one until such times as I was free to get my own.

Glenn was a great dog! He was good fun, very clever and easy to train. I couldn't wait to get him chasing things once he was obedient enough to be trusted to come back after the game had escaped or he had caught it. Our secret training sessions away from the village in the woods and fields proved him to have a good nose, a gutsy determination and a fairly good turn of speed for a big, thick set dog.

I caught a few rabbits with him and was elated. I felt so happy and distracted from things when we were out and about mooching around, this laid the foundation for me looking once again through the free ads newspapers shortly after I got my first house aged 17. I barely had a scrap of furniture or possessions to my name but the minute I had enough money to buy a dog I bought one. She cost me £40 from an old gypsy man and he spat on his hand and gave me a pound back "for luck"

I definitely needed it as she was useless!

Headstrong, selectively deaf, could run all day but didn't catch anywhere near as much as she should have for her shape or the way she was bred. All in all a very frustrating dog but I was determined the next one would be better and he was. The next one after him was a bit better again and soon I was regularly out and about in the hills around my new home catching rabbits and hares. I read books from the local library about ferrets and ferreting and bought some of those too. Next came the lamp and I started lamping. That's hunting at night time with a powerful torch for anyone not too aghast at the subject material, who's still reading. My days often consisted of ferreting in the morning, either having a packed lunch or walking home for a bite to eat, then shooting around dusk time when there would always be more rabbits around, then lamping at night when most normal people were in bed. Oh how I wish I had the youthful energy now that I had back then!

I've tried many times to describe the rush of endorphins you get when you're out working your dogs or shooting in the countryside, whether it's running a lurcher or shooting over a gundog there's a deep rooted satisfaction at the end of a good day's sport that makes you feel connected to the land, especially when you dress and cook the game yourself for dinner which was something I always enjoyed doing. I think you can either grasp this or you can't - it's very hard to tell someone how sporting hobbies make you feel, they're something you have to experience to understand fully. Many people are too closed-minded to even give it a try.

I started writing articles about my exploits and getting paid for them which was a novelty for me. Lots of other people enjoyed the same hobby and I began to make friends who were into the same things. We would hunt or shoot together then have a good drink afterwards, a bit of food and dissection of the day's activities, teasing each other about who had the worst dog (usually me!) or the funniest thing that happened that day. One of my favourite fieldsports friends had a contract to provide rabbits to feed the tigers and other large carnivores at Glasgow Zoo, so we would go all out to help the farmers rid their land of vermin and he earned a good wee wage out of it. Somewhere along the line I was invited to a party where lots of doggy folk got together and as the guests filtered into the room my gaze fell and fixated on one man in particular who was to shake up my world in various ways.

We didn't get together that night, he was with a blonde woman who was practically grinding her crotch into his face and trying everything to get him to notice her, but he was as fixated on me as I was on him. We chatted to other people throughout the night, him at one side of the room with the guys, me on the other side with the women, but we couldn't stop looking at each other in between. I had heard a lot about this man, he had a reputation for being both a womaniser and having the best dogs around which was a potent combination. He had heard a lot about me too. A young, attractive, slightly mad woman who also liked hunting, shooting and dogs wasn't all that common back in the day so I think as well as having intense sexual chemistry from across a crowded room, we were both intrigued by one another.

At one point he beckoned me across, I stood up to go over and chat and it honestly felt like the music stopped playing, the room turned to watch what was going to happen next and everything started to move in slow motion. I noticed one guy nudge another and give a look as if to say "Oh aye here we go" Then there was blondie, she was giving me looks that could kill, I better not go near her man! He wasn't her man of course he was someone else's man entirely. I knew he was married. I'd been told and well warned.

Warnings always had the opposite effect on me (and my shoulder pal Devil), like a red flag to a bull, but somehow as drunk as I was, Angel voice kicked in and told me to turn round and sit back down. I obeyed, sat back down and he continued looking at me, his stare piercing my soul, he looked quizzical and disappointed, yet more intrigued than before. I decided I would wait until he went to the toilet and make a move then, so we'd meet in the hallway and be able to chat privately, but the man was seemingly a camel and didn't move all night. I got so drunk at one point I went to the toilet and another doggy guy was in there, I ended up throwing up in the sink beside him. The next thing I know we are getting off with each other up against the toilet door. Angel voice is nagging "What are you doing? This isn't the man you want, mind you the state you're in you should stay well away from men full stop!" I come to my senses and push him away. His trousers are around his ankles and he has a tiny cock, I laugh and leave him standing there.

When I return to the party blondie has Mr Man firmly in her grip, she's on his lap giving him a lap dance so I give up and other than the occasional lingering glance at each other, I eventually fall asleep. When I wake in the morning my friend who's hosted the party has kindly covered me with a blanket, and Mr Man is gone.

But not for long!

He arrives at my house within a few weeks with a mutual hunting friend to introduce us properly. It's a quaintly old fashioned, very thinly veiled attempt to pretend they are just passing by and thought they would call in to say "Hello"

I sense straight away that what he really wants is to dispense with the middleman and get to know me on a one-on-one basis at the first opportunity. It's written all over his face and in his body language. I've not been any good at hiding my intentions up until now so I'm probably giving off the same vibe in return.

I'm immediately drawn to him, I described it to a friend as a magnetic forcefield I was powerless to resist, and we strike up an odd friendship over the next 6 months where we have the best, most amazing hunting and shooting trips, the best laughs and the most sexual tension I've ever felt towards anyone in my life up until that point.

I had finally found someone with the same passion as me, on the same wavelength who I found irresistibly attractive. Angel is nagging away telling me to be careful! He's married and your spending way too much time together. It doesn't matter that nothing has happened between you, you know it's only a matter of time! Remember the story of King David and how he lusted after Bathsheba. If he had only looked away instead of bringing her to his bedroom, all the lives that could have been spared. It doesn't matter how much of a sham his marriage is or how it's one of convenience in name only, they still made vows to each other, most likely in front of God. Remember him? The all seeing, all knowing one who's been judging your entire descent down the express elevator straight to hell. Every time you go hunting or shooting together, it's behind his wife's back. She plagues me with pangs of guilt sprinkled with the word adulteress. It's not a label I ever thought I would be branded with. The chemistry is getting stronger and stronger though and Devil is saying life is short! Make the most of it. Soulmates don't come along very often, how can you miss this opportunity? Even if he's not your soul mate who cares? Think of all the sexy, sexual, sexy, sex!

His dogs are better than mine, which isn't hard to be honest. All of my dogs bar one, before I met him, I'd tried to take short cuts to success by bargain basement shopping for adult dogs, perpetually changing hands on the awful carousel that was the free ad press. They definitely have a better home when they come home to live with me, one poor dog was skin and bones and living in a chicken coop when I went to buy her, but I know deep down a well-bred puppy is what I need. Starting from scratch with a clean slate. Good parents coupled with good rearing gives a good head start. Then it's up to me to train and enter the youngster and nurse it along until it's an invaluable member of the team. His dogs are bred from a long line of good workers, more exciting to watch than mine and he gives me a puppy as a present, and then another. They were to form the foundation of the line of dogs I still have to this day.

Dogs aside though, tension between us is brewing and Angel and Devil are about to have a huge battle on my shoulders. We have a particularly great day out one day and he suggests coming up for a wee drink one night. This is him testing the water to see if I'll let him spend the night. I say "Yeah, Sure" and instantly both regret it and feel overwhelmingly excited at the prospect of finally feeling his lips on mine and him plunged deep inside me for the first time. Normally I wonder about a man's size and girth, but with him the thought doesn't even come into my mind, I just know it's all going to be good. The fact he doesn't mention it makes me feel quietly confident. The men who mention it a lot are usually the ones who are sadly lacking in that department so it plays heavily on their mind.

There's been so many times it felt like we were about to kiss but didn't. He comments all the time about how crazy it is to find a girl who's on a different level competing squarely with all the guys in what is essentially a male dominated sport.

I love my solo hunting and shooting trips and my days and nights out with my other hunting friends but really, I want to spend them with him more than anyone else. Field sports have become our foreplay. The exciting appetiser before the main course which is him finally cornering me, his prey, and getting to devour me, or vice versa as I'm beginning to wonder why he doesn't make a move when the vibe is so palpable between us.

Eventually he asks me if there's anything between me and my male friend who hosted the party where we met. I explain "Nope we're just hunting buddies" To which he replies he wouldn't be able to hide how he felt and would have put his cards on the table by now. Then there's the longest silence ever and the usual intense stare between us where it feels like we're undressing each other in our minds. Angel scolds Devil "don't you dare put your cards on the table! This one's dangerous so caution is needed! Better still he shouldn't even be here, you should stop this before you reach the point of no return!"

I've had butterflies in my stomach every time I think about him or see him for months now and I don't think I can take much more of it. We have such a good laugh and banter every time we go out. What's the worst that can happen?

Chapter 10

Horny Part II

Spoiler Alert : This chapter contains coarse language and depictions of sexual activity. Please do skip it if you think it'll be triggering. Before writing this book, I researched the reviews section of other books I had read and was dismayed to see people leaving negative reviews for writers who mention far less than I am about to. If you have happened upon this book under some misconception it is going to be frilly hearts and flowers, you are sadly mistaken. I would rather you gave it to a broad minded friend to enjoy instead, than lambasting me online for being truthful about my life.

A torrid affair has begun. It starts the night he comes to mine for a drink. We sit politely together on the sofa chatting about dogs and general small talk, but I feel like I'm going to literally explode if I don't have him inside me soon. I go to the toilet to gather my thoughts and take a long hard look at myself in the mirror. Angel speaks as loudly to me as though another person was in the room.

"You can't do this! You mustn't do this! It's wrong! Is this really the sort of person you want to be? He's married. You don't want to have an affair with a married man, You know this is wrong, you've only got a short while to stop this before nature takes its course. Feel how wet you are for fuck sake!" Angel never swears so I know this time she means business.

I have a feel and I've never been this wet before. I'm throbbing so hard inside it feels like my womb is trying to escape through my belly button.

I rehearse in my head what I'm going to say to call the evening to a halt. There's not much time to stop this before the point of no return, I can't conceal it any longer. I decide I'll tell him I'm really sorry but I can't do this. I don't want to get involved with a married man and he needs to go home because I'm starting to catch feelings for him. I'd rather stop things before they go any further and end the night on a good note. I've had a really nice time but what we're doing is shady and we both know it. It sounds good in my head. Angel is proud of me, Devil is suspiciously silent.

I return to the living room and sit back down beside him. He smells a bit like shortbread biscuits baking, a delicious warm, sweet smell, so appetising. I honestly want to eat him up starting with his face and finishing with his crotch. The conversation has died a death, we're staring at each other and all of a sudden Devil blurts out "Are we going to sit here and talk about dogs all night?"

For a split second the thought enters my mind that I'm not entirely in control of anything I'm doing here and that Angel and Devil are pulling my strings like a puppet. I'm just dancing to their respective tunes, my actions and speech completely directed by whichever one manages to overpower the other at any given moment.

What a terrifying thought!

I know what Mum would have to say about it all. It's been a few years now since she disowned me due to my sinful life course, but I can still hear her lectures rumbling around in my mind like distant thunderstorms. JW's are very fond of harping on about the world being surrounded by invisible spirit beings called demons who have been cast down to earth. Condemned to an eventual fiery destruction, they have a short period of time to unleash their wicked desires on humanity. They are portrayed as evil masters of corruption and pain infliction. Their speciality is either invading and controlling people by entering their bodies, or getting people to perform all sorts of sexual perversions because they enjoy watching humans have sex.

I don't have time to indulge this train of thought, as no sooner than it enters my head, my tongue enters his mouth and we're entwined, I'm scrambling on top of him, can't get my legs open fast enough, he's ripping my clothes off, squeezing my breasts, kissing me all over. I'm tearing at his clothes with equal intensity. No going back now then! We don't have time for foreplay, we've waited what seemed like an eternity already, and he's inside me, telling me it's so, so good. We're copulating frantically like a pair of wild animals in a race to devour each other's bodies. We lie in a panting heap afterwards and the minute he recovers we're at it again, the next time is amazing, having burst quickly out of the gate the first time round, he now takes his sweet time, pushing and pulling me around into some positions I've only ever seen in the Kama Sutra. I'm not naturally the most flexible person, but he has me rolling

around and bending to his demands like I'm
made of plasticine. Every successive move or
thrust he makes elicits louder and more urgent
squeals from me and I find myself gasping in
shock at how good this sex thing can actually be
when you do it with someone you really fancy!
He's the best lover I've had so far. I'm hooked,
no return from this deviant path now. We
embark on a long and sordid few years of
rampant sex, indoors, outdoors, anywhere we
feel like it. Sometimes when we're out in the
fields and hills, other times he'll come round just
to rip my clothes off the minute he gets in the
door, we can't get enough of each other. We love
to do it in risky places where there's a slight
chance we might get caught. He loves to bend
me over things when we're outdoors and I love
taking every throbbing inch of him.

After a while though, Angel starts to really gnaw
away at me, I feel restless and annoyed and I
want more, I deserve more. It's not like me to
be second best to anyone, to accept another
woman's scraps. I've ended relationships for far
less in the past. I haven't pushed for us to be
together properly but soon the chance arises.
His wife finds out about another affair he had
many years ago. He pays child maintenance to

the woman for the children, secretly through his sister so his wife won't find out. The saying I heard when I first came into the doggy circle seems to be true, that he's a womaniser who's got loads of kids to different women all around the area where he lives. He has an argument about it with his middle son, the son tells his mother and all hell breaks loose. I think this is our chance to be together and for a very short while we are, and I'm happy, it feels very natural, but he soon informs me he has to go back, he wants to go back, he hates being away from his dogs, his other two sons and the house is his, passed down to him from his mother when she died. He doesn't want to get screwed over and end up with nothing. I feel crushed. If it wasn't bad enough feeling like I was doing something really bad by being with someone else's man, now he was choosing bricks and mortar over me. We row, we break up, I try to have relationships with other men, but nobody else comes close, nobody makes me feel the way he does so I keep getting caught in a cycle of bouncing back to him for a few years until finally Angel wins, her nagging has paid off, I'm done! I really do deserve so much better. He doesn't love me, he just loves the sex and the escape from his mundane life for a few hours. I feel thoroughly ashamed of myself and vow if I'm ever in this sort of situation again I will listen to Angel immediately and just say NO.

Shortly before we split for good, I meet a girl at a party in the local pub. She gets up on stage and sings and I'm mesmerised by her, she's very attractive, confident, a great singer, I'm immediately drawn to her. Halfway through the night she walks past and I smile and tell her she was great up there. It turns out one of her Aunt's is the new owner of the local pub, she's going to be coming to sing at functions now and then, so we agree to meet up sometime for a drink. When we do, the conversation flows really naturally and I find myself back to the Suzie situation. Except this time I reckon I'm not going to be able to shelve or dodge these feelings, I need to know for my own curiosities sake if I'm bisexual, bi-curious, lesbian or whatever shade of grey in between.

She seems to hang around with quite a lot of lesbians so I ask her straight out if she is one. (I'm nosey remember!) She laughs and tells me no, people always think that but her aunts are lesbians and she just feels comfortable because she's grown up around them. She says she's often thought about trying it but never found the right person. She then asks me the same and my heart skipping a beat or two, I tell her about Suzie - about how I liked her as more than just a friend in High School. I tell her about the night we went clubbing when she was at Uni, we left her boyfriend at home and she came on to me in the club but I freaked out a bit and didn't reciprocate. I felt bad for her boyfriend but was also worried that it might affect our friendship, but then that became a bit odd and strained anyway after that night so I often wished I had been courageous enough to just go for it and see if I liked it.

Not long after this revelation I hear a knock at my door one night and there she is, all dolled up, looking mighty fine, bottle of cider in hand, did I fancy getting it on? She had obviously had a few already for Dutch courage and I was stone cold sober so I tell her look let's go to the pub for a couple of drinks and a chat and see where we go from there. Devil is bawling at me to take her straight to the bedroom and unleash my inner lesbo. But, for once I decide to be sensible. This feels like a big thing so I need to be sure. Of course nowadays it's nothing at all and there's so many new dimensions than just

straight, bi and gay there's every sort of mixture
of everything else you could possibly imagine,
but back then this was a big deal.

A few drinks later and I'm ready, I whisper
cheekily, "Ok, let's do this" so we slip away into
the night for a kiss and it's actually really lovely,
I'm enjoying it far more than I thought I would.
I like it so much I panic a little and say that I
think we should be careful 'cos it's a small
village and we don't want anyone to know what
were up to until we figure it out ourselves. She
agrees, we kiss again but as we do we can hear
voices at the door. There's a glass panel in the
main wooden door to the pub and as we gasp
for air after a very passionate kiss and look
towards the door, there is my next door
neighbour, who couldn't keep a secret if his life
depended on it, he's laughing and pointing and
thinking this is great! We laugh about it too and
decide well that's that out of the window now, if
the whole village is going to be talking about us,
which knowing my neighbour will be in about
ten minutes time, we may as well just go the
whole way rather than just kiss and then at least
the rumours will be true.

We slink off to her place and enjoy a night of unbridled lust where we fondle each other's breasts, kiss a lot and eventually end up in her bed, naked, exploring each other's bodies. Tentatively at first, but steadily getting bolder, I bury my face between her thighs and lick her until she orgasms. Girls are much nicer to kiss than guys let me tell you this in case you've never tried it, and boobs are nice too, it felt nice to play with a pair which were much bigger than mine, I always wanted bigger ones having been teased so much at school for being flat as a pancake. "Bee Stings" was one of my nicknames. If the school bullies could see me now they would have a field day! We were both very turned on and I decided I had to give this a try to see if I was a lesbian or not. A couple of minutes in and I knew for sure I wasn't but I didn't have the heart to say anything or screech to a sudden halt in my activities, especially since she was enjoying it so much. So I made a rather heroic effort of making a woman who wasn't me orgasm for the first time and then we collapsed in a heap together, spent.

I felt a bit odd as we lay together cuddling. It was nice don't get me wrong but I had an overwhelming urge to get up and leave now that it was all over. Angel was saying all sorts of things about how dirty and sinful I was, I'd really gone and crossed the line now! Devil was laughing, high fiving me and saying this is what a man feels like when he's had casual, meaningless sex. He's happy and satisfied and just wants out of there. I lie there feeling bad for quite a while until eventually she's in a deep enough sleep for me to sneak away without waking her. I have done the "walk of shame" home from the pub many times in the past, it's a village joke that you have to walk past all the gossip's houses to get home. They sit there all night twitching their curtains to see who's doing what so they have something fresh to tell everyone the next day. I chuckle at the thought of what tomorrow's topic will be.

I'm sort of glad I do it, as it feels like I needed to, to confirm that I'm actually primarily straight and I much prefer men. I do still find her attractive, I'm not entirely repulsed at what we did and I wouldn't be opposed to some top half play again in the future, especially if a certain man was involved! We're doomed to failure and the expiration date is well past on our "relationship" so I figure a three-way might be quite a nice way to go out with a bang. Devil gives this plan a massive thumbs up.

Fortunately she feels the same way and tells me the next time we meet that while the other night was fun, she doesn't want to be a lesbian either. She thinks we should just use our newfound fun fling as an appetiser for the main meal which of course for both of us is cock, preferably a nice big one, that we can share and play together with. What should feel like a rejection, even though I planned to say something similar, is a massive turn on so I tell her all about my soon to be ex. She meets him, is up for it, perhaps not today though? But definitely sometime in the near future. I'm excited at the prospect. So is Mr Man. He says he's never had a threesome and would love to have one before he's too old and past it.

Note to self : Men always say this even if they are gangbang experts and they are NEVER too old. A man will have a three-way on his deathbed if the nurses are up for it.

It's not to be though, a short time later she meets a guy, falls in love and ends up moving away. Life seems to have this way of constantly short changing me on so many fronts. Angel triumphantly says this is a good thing, having mind blowing sex with two of my favourite people would only prolong the already doomed "relationship" longer as I'm too greedy to be content with one good session. If it's good I want seconds, and thirds....

Devil says "You stupid bitch why didn't you just go over, take his cock out and start sucking it in front of her. She would have joined in for sure. You've only yourself to blame for missing your one and only opportunity"

I break up with Mr Man for good, it's long overdue, and now I'm left with a gapingly large hole which I know I'm wasting my time trying to fill with other men. I try and fail many times, they aren't big enough, they don't look, smell or taste as nice as him, they don't do it the way he did it or for as long. Their banter is rubbish and none of them give me that sickly butterfly feeling he did. Every time I try, I lie there afterwards feeling stupid, used, dirty, fed up. Each time I tell myself I'm going to use them, but I always end up feeling like they get the last laugh. I decide to listen to Angel and have a wee break for a bit to get my head together.

A local woman is selling a pony as it kicks and bites, her kids she bought it for are terrified of it, and this seems like a good, wholesome way to distract myself from things, so I agree to buy him, even though I haven't much of a clue about how to ride him, where to keep him? It feels like the right thing to do though and I'm glad I make this choice because if you're trying to forget about having a big, powerful male between your legs, this is one of the very best substitutes.

Chapter 11

Horses

Let me tell you something, horses are amazing animals!

The very fact they allow humans, an apex predator to sit astride them is a miracle of nature. Horses in the wild are vulnerable to attack by killing machines such as lions trying to jump onto their backs and maul them. Or gangs of canids such as wolves which will attack in packs, going for sensitive areas such as the nose, tail and genitals, to slow them down to a standstill. The remainder of the pack will then overwhelm them to the ground, disembowel and begin eating while the horse is still alive. Nature is cruel and shocking and this is the reality of a wild horse's existence. They survive by moving in herds and being swift in their escape as well as having a protective arsenal of large teeth, strong hooves and a brave spirit.

Everything is a potential threat to a horse. I'm showing my age here but a ribbon from a discarded tape is viewed the same way a poisonous snake lying in waiting to strike might be. A flapping bag stuck in a fence could be a predator about to jump out. That loud bang could be the distant roar of a lion about to attack.

It really is something then to think we are able to tame them to the extent they trust us to put metal in their mouth, leather across their backs and noses, around their necks, underbelly and in some cases their tail.

The dog is widely regarded as man's best friend but the horse is definitely his best helper. Carrying warriors into battle, pulling chariots, providing food and hides and in some cultures milk, the horse powered the human world for so long we still refer to them today when summarising a car's engine capacity.

This period of my life is a very calm, settled and tranquil one. I once read somewhere that horses help to stabilise a woman's mood and hormones. I don't know the truth of this statement but it really resonated with me. Horses have definitely healed me. The constant negative inner monologue and opposing Angel and Devil voices fall relatively silent during the next few years as I become completely absorbed with my new hobby. I read and watch anything I can get my hands on which is horse related, gleaning every last morsel of useful information. Funnily enough one of the most interesting books I read is by my childhood heroine Barbara Woodhouse, who turned out not to just be an amazing dog trainer but also a pretty good horse woman too. I learn everything I can about horses, I'm like a sponge soaking it all up, trying to cram as much knowledge as possible in so I can be best equipped to ride, groom, look after and feed my new best friend.

I also meet a nice man and try hard to have a "normal" relationship. He's lovely, but sadly it doesn't work out. Nobody can replace Mr Man there's just not anybody out there good enough looking, or good enough in bed or who looks at me the way he used to. He used to look at me like I was a tasty dish he wanted to devour. So we end up just like two good pals rather than boyfriend and girlfriend and that's fine. Men are like shoes you have to try on lots of pairs before you find the perfect fit, the ones that feel as comfortable as slippers.

I fill my time with my horse or should I say horses, as just like dogs, chickens and tattoos, it's virtually impossible to just have one. They like company and if you have the space it really makes sense to have two or three or even more.

Sadly, like all good things eventually it comes to an end, I'm finding it a struggle to afford to keep him, he's having problems with his back, most likely exacerbated by me being a terrible rider with awful posture rolling around up there like a sack of tatties. Eventually I come to the reluctant decision to rehome him to a children's riding school which absolutely breaks my heart and leaves me once again with a huge, aching, empty hole.

I despair and wonder if anything is ever going to go right for me in life? Everything seems so fleeting. I'm beginning to learn that good things must be grasped tightly with both hands as they just don't last.

I often look back fondly on this time period in my life though and wish I could rewind back into it. I was much fitter as horse riding really strengthens your core and helps your posture as well as being amazing fun and totally exhilarating. I was far happier those few short years than I ever was before or afterwards, but life had a way of always coming to crossroads and leaving me standing wondering which fork to take. Angel and Devil begin to wrestle with each other over which path I should take next. It didn't help that those pesky little critters hormones were playing a powerful part in dictating my actions. Fast running out of ovaries, my hormones were driving me to try to find a new Mr Man and fill that gaping void that most "normal" people fill with satisfying careers, marriage, children etc. I on the other hand was being driven by a teeny tiny pair of internal organs screaming "Make babies quick"

Translated into Angel's voice, knowing my complete disdain for the idea of having children, she whispered quietly "Maybe it's time to either settle down with a nice man or dedicate your life to something meaningful"

All the while Devil voice kept goading me to fuck the brains out of every good looking guy I came across.

Chapter 12

Hormones

As a post-menopausal lady fast approaching 50, I can now with complete confidence and hindsight say that hormones are a real bitch!

As much as we need those delightful little amounts of oestrogen and progesterone coursing around our bloodstreams to keep us happy, healthy and fertile, they can also be the bane of our lives, leading us to make poor choices when it comes to male sexual partners and life choices in general.

It's a scientific fact that when a heterosexual woman is ovulating she will display visual and scent-determined preferences for males with more symmetrical, masculine facial features. Some studies even go as far as to suggest during this short period of fertility and receptivity women are likely to prefer men other than their current partner. This is often referred to as the "Good Genes Theory"

I also have my own personal theory based on nothing scientific at all which tells me that every woman has only a limited supply of eggs to last her lifetime. So, if like me, you started early and have a short menstrual cycle, you could find yourself firing out eggs like one of those Japanese Ping Pong Girls. I had my first period in primary school, way before any of my female classmates. My cycle as well as being monstrously painful each month was incredibly short, sometimes as little as 20 or 22 days so I could often have 2 periods in the same calendar month.

For me personally, I experienced this as being perpetually horny from my teens right through until my late 30's, making some truly horrendous sexual partner choices based entirely on what my hormones were telling me to do. My internal monologue war raged between Angel and Devil, Angel was mainly over ruled as Devil wielded oestrogen and ovulation as a powerful pitch fork!

There was a constant battle raging between them, Angel telling me to just find one nice man and settle down, try to act like a normal person because deep down all this casual sex was not good for me, my reputation or my potential eternal soul. Devil wanted me to fuck my way across the county, having the wildest times I could so that in my dotage at least I would have some interesting memories to look back on.

It's funny the way attraction works. As a teenager and in my 20's I found boys my own age immature, unbearable and a complete turn off, I vastly preferred an older man. Mr Man who I had an on – off intense relationship with in my 20's was 20 years older than me. Psychologists would probably attempt to say this was because I had deep rooted "Daddy Issues" and maybe they were right, but I just enjoyed sex more with a mature, confident, experienced man.

This all began to change in my 30's. Whatever wonderful things were happening in my ovaries, they began whispering to me that there was this whole untapped generation of younger men out there just waiting to be explored. Suddenly the oldies held less appeal and I entered a cougar phase which is one I reminisce on both giggling and cringing in equal measures.

There was a woman lived locally at the time who had the nickname "Mrs Up 'N' Doon Drawers" and we hung out together sometimes. She was a good drinking buddy, good fun and held some great parties when the pub closed for the night and everyone wanted to carry on partying. As much fun as this all was, I started to be plagued by Angel nagging at me that she was the talk of the place and I was fast following in her footsteps.

I made excuses for her saying that she had been in a long marriage which had come to an end, she was simply having some fun and letting her hair down to catch up on all those years she missed out. The trouble is if you live in a small village you can't really get away with having multiple partners and no backlash. It's different if you live in a city where there's much more scope for anonymity.

Crossroads time came when I walked into my local one day to find a few folk giggling and giving me funny looks. They soon caved and showed me what was so funny. Someone had spotted a profile on a swingers site, a really filthy one, with our village named as the hometown. It was just a photo of her breasts and hairline but they had collectively decided it was either me or Mrs Up 'N' Doon Drawers. To be fair to the landlady she had kindly pointed out I was much younger skinned than the woman in the picture and jumped to my defence. I then had to go through the ribbing of everyone else teasing me while trying to explain that my boobs weren't that big for starters. The woman in the photo had darker hair and despite me liking sex, I don't like doing any of the things she said she liked to do in her profile!

Angel gnawed away at me for the millionth time saying "Right enough is enough, if your determined to be a sex maniac which you clearly are, why not find a nice, decent man, settle down with him and get as much sex as you want without ending up a laughing stock like your tarty friend here"

Devil said "How boring!" and went on to point out the many comparisons between us, I was younger and better looking and the men I was sleeping with were much better looking, so anyone who had anything bad to say must just be jealous! Devil likes comparisons. It's easier to justify something if you compare yourself to someone who's "worse" than you.

Then a well-meaning friend said she was worried I was getting a reputation as she overheard a couple of guys talking about us in derogatory terms, more so her than me, but still, not nice to hear. Angel took this and ran with it, making me decide there and then to listen to her advice.

I would try online dating sites and see if I could meet someone nice. I would play by "The Rules" not being too eager or flirty, not using sex as though it were the only thing I had of interest or value, even if somewhere deep down this was how I often felt. I could have great and meaningful conversations about all sorts with men I didn't find attractive and they would admire my wit and intellect. But put a tall, dark, handsome man in front of me and my ovaries would turn me into a silly, twittering mess.

An overhaul of my entire dating structure was required. As usual, book nerd that I am I read lots of books and articles on how to look, dress and act my best. Mrs Up 'N' Doon Drawers having humped her way round the village had now moved away down south, no doubt to continue her sexual adventures where there was plenty of fresh meat, so I had no bad influences to egg on Devil's desires.

It wasn't easy to find someone though!

I spent a year on one popular site and only went on two dates, one with a man who was obsessed with talking about his ex-wife and was as camp as a row of tents. By the end of our date I could see why she had left him. He was so far back in the closet he was in Narnia. My other date was with a man who looked and sounded lovely in our online chat but had missing teeth and camel breath when we met in person.

I met a couple of other guys on a different dating site. One had the cold, scary eyes of a psychopath to such an extent I spoke to him for ten minutes in the car park and then hastily made an excuse so I wouldn't actually have to go inside and have a drink with him. Funnily enough many years later I met and became friends with a lovely lady who spent 3 years with this man and he verbally and physically abused her so I consider this one a lucky escape!

After a couple of years of this trying to be the "best me I possibly could be" and really trying to put myself out there, I was almost ready to give up. I would delete my profiles and then after a week or two panic and think what if my "Mr Right" had joined while I was absent and we missed each other like ships in the night?

I would go back on them and find all that was in my inbox were the same shady, ugly, boring, predictable men that were there the last time I looked. They became a sea of depressing faces staring blankly back at me. Just as I was about to give up for good, one face in particular stood out.

We'd chatted a bit on an online dog site and I had made plans to use his stud dog on one of my girls. For some reason, based on his terrible spelling, punctuation and way of expressing himself I had formed an image in my mind of a dishevelled old Irishman with grey, bushy sprouting hair, including from his ears and nostrils. I deduced that I'd have to stand well back from him when we did finally meet to mate the dogs, as he would have a pungent, farmery smell to him. He would likely have trousers held up with baler twine and be unpleasant to have to endure in my inbox until the dastardly doggy deed had taken place.

A photo appeared of him online with said dog and I was taken aback. He was nothing like the image I'd conjured, not strictly my type as such as I do like tall, dark and handsome, but he was 1 out of the 3 and despite being balding with short cropped greying hair he did look very well in the picture. Something else was also playing a

part, something I probably should have
mentioned in a previous chapter but didn't, so
buckle up your belts for our next time jump!

Chapter 13

Hypnagogic

Dreams have always held a great fascination for me.

We spend approximately 30% of our lives either sleeping, or trying to get to sleep, which equates to roughly 1 third of our lifespan, 26 years sleeping and 7 trying to get to sleep. Having suffered from both hypersomnia (sleeping too much) and insomnia (not being able to get to sleep) at different stages of my life, as well as something referred to as the "Tetris Effect" it has always puzzled me why we don't have more research on the subject or dedicate more time to studying something which is such a massive part of our lives.

It's the kind of thing we take for granted, a bit like breathing or blinking, until one day there's an issue with our sleep pattern such as falling asleep when we want to be awake, or not being able to sleep when we need to.

The most intriguing of all have been the prophetic and recurring dreams I've experienced throughout my life. I don't know if it's a genetic thing as my Mum in her pre JW days often told me about recurring dreams she had.

Of course the Bible is jam packed with freaky dream stuff. God used dreams so many times to warn people of impending doom, reveal hidden meanings in things and help them make life changing decisions. Perhaps because of this both my Mum and I placed more importance on dreams than your average person? She felt as though some dreams were warnings and premonitions of future events.

Her most notable one she shared with me involved a doctor in a white coat chasing her with a knife. Years later when she had me, she felt it had come true because upon waking after a long, difficult and very painful labour, the doctor told her she had just escaped his knife, in other words I was born naturally after initially presenting in the wrong position. She had been sent down to have a c-section but I had other plans and turned around, making a bolt for the exit at the last minute.

Perhaps this influenced me to place more importance on dreams than necessary? Or maybe some people are predisposed to having vivid dreams which have a deeper meaning. Who knows? But they have become a regular feature in my life which through time, trial and error I have learned to note them, learn from them and let them speak to me and guide me. You wouldn't be reading this book and I wouldn't have written it if not for my most recent prophetic dream.

The first time I experienced an unusual dream was as a child. I didn't make sense of it until some 40 odd years later which feels like quite a long wait for not very much in return, but others I've had since, their meaning has become clear much faster.

My recurring dream consisted of a shadowy figure wearing a soldier's helmet and cape standing atop a hill. I kept having it and asked my Mum what it meant. She told me dreams are mostly what we've eaten before bedtime and whatever is trapped in our subconscious mind when we fall asleep which is a pretty good explanation really.

As the saying goes "Sweet dreams are made of Cheese.

Who am I to dis a Brie?

I Cheddar the world

And the Feta cheese

Every bodies looking for Stilton"

I chalked it down to eating too much of my favourite food. As we were not a wealthy household and mealtimes were already fairly sparse with my mum struggling to feed a large family, I deemed it best not to mention my Spartan friend again in case the rations we were already on became even more meagre.

As it happened many years later when I met my current partner he told me about his favourite rock band and I immediately recognised the iconic figure from their album cover. I most likely saw it on telly and without paying much attention to it the cheese latched onto the image and regurgitated it for me as a vivid dream. After the chat with my Mum I never had it again. How odd! I do get a warm fuzzy glow though having been to see the band in adulthood, meeting them afterwards and getting my album signed. I'm not sure what this all means in the grand scheme of things but seeing my prophetic dreams through to completion so they make sense in some way has become a bit of a hobby of mine.

The next oddity occurred a few years later when I began experiencing the Tetris Effect. First as a result of growing up in a household where my elder brother was an avid gamer and game creator. This was in the early 80's and things were vastly different back then. Modern game designers would laugh their heads off at the games we thought were so cutting edge. They would likely look like morse code dots and dashes by comparison to the high tech 3D graphics and surround sound of today's games.

Nevertheless, I was the game playing guinea pig, an annoying little sister has her uses. He would create the games and I would play them. Helping him identify glitches in the code and improve each level. I would often play for hours until my fingers and thumbs hurt or my Mum would yell at me that my time was up, I had homework to do or it was bedtime.

This is when the Tetris Effect came into play, way before the game Tetris itself had ever been invented. Basically it means you continue to experience something as you sleep, or fall asleep that you were immersed in before you went to bed. So a skier might feel snow beneath their feet as they drift off or a chess player might see the board and move the pieces as they sleep.

I would often find it hard to switch off from game playing and would experience the game continuing long after I'd gone to bed. My normal dreams would be replaced with synthetic feeling graphics and sound and I always woke up the next day feeling as though I hadn't actually slept properly.

It wasn't just gaming either. I suffered a lot of social awkwardness and anxiety as a youngster. Living in a small rural village there wasn't much in the way of things to do for kids, especially in winter time, so there were few opportunities outwith school for me to improve my confidence. I would attend various events at the local village hall including badminton and when I came home to bed I found it difficult to switch off. It were as though my mind was processing

the entire night's events. I was so socially
awkward I was unable to whilst I was awake. I
would often wake up sitting upright in bed
having full blown conversations with people
thinking I was playing badminton or carpet
bowls, another rural pastime which was boring
as hell but one of the few ways you got to mix
with other folk your own age and older.
Sometimes I would wake having a panic attack
that everyone in the hall would see me in my
pyjamas, then I would come around to full
consciousness and realise I was in bed and the
whole thing was just a dream. Sometimes my
Mum would wake up and come to check I was
OK and who was I talking to at 3am?

On the rare occasions I stayed at friend's houses
it was always worse as I was more likely to
sleepwalk too if I was in an unfamiliar
environment. One night at a friend's sleepover I
got up in the middle of the night and started
dressing, shouting at everyone to hurry up or we
would miss the school bus. It was Sunday and I
had been trying to put my friend's trousers over
my head thinking it was a jumper. Much hilarity
and piss taking ensued.

In my 20's the weird dreams definitely calmed a little and settled into 4 distinct groups.

Number 1 I call "normal" food or conversation related dreams whereby you tend to dream about something you've watched, listened to or been talking to someone about shortly before bed. Ever wake up with a song in your head and its stuck there for the whole day? That happened to me so, so much!

Number 2 I call vivid dreams which really stand out from the normal ones. They will feel so real, colourful and filled with emotion that you might wake up feeling elated, disturbed, happy or sad depending on the dream content. These dreams are like going to see a really dramatic movie in 3D as opposed to just a normal run of the mill film at home.

Number 3 I call prophetic. As soon as you have one of these dreams you know it means something, you just have to work out what and why. Sometimes this takes a long time (Spartan soldier for example) sometimes things reveal themselves very fast in a matter of days, weeks or months rather than years.

Number 4 I call Deja Reve which is where you dream about something or someone and then the thing happens or you meet the person in real life.

These are by far the freakiest of all!

Technically there is also Number 5 which is lucid dreaming whereby using a process of repetitive daytime counting or reality check activities, you are then able to determine whilst sleeping that you are in fact dreaming. As a result of this revelation you then begin to control, direct and more actively enjoy and participate in the dream than just being a bystander or viewer.

I really tried to become a lucid dreamer at one point in my 30's but I found the repetitive finger counting or pressing tedious, I never seemed to master the art of doing it anytime I was asleep so I gave up. I was only ever lucid once, for the briefest of moments. I was flying a plane, something I'm terrified of in my waking state, so I realised I was dreaming, felt overwhelmingly elated and then promptly lost control, crashed the plane and woke up in my excitement. Sometimes I think I should give it another go and see what happens.

The spartan soldier childhood dream I can explain away into category Number 1, but in my 20's I had a dream one night which fell most distinctly into Category 4.

It wasn't anything spectacular, just a normal seeming dream but there was a good looking guy in it with dark hair who kept catching my eye. I kept thinking, who's he? He's a bit shorter than my usual type but he looks nice. Why's he here if I don't know who he is? Normally we tend to dream about people we know, places that are familiar to us. I woke wondering who the mystery man was, then promptly dismissed it and forgot all about him.

Until a few months later when I heard a knock at the door and there he was. I still chuckle to this day at how I must have come across. He was a friend of Mr Man and had heard I had some ferrets for sale. I just stood there open mouthed, speechless thinking what the....??

Devil really wanted me to blurt out "You're the dude from my dream!" but fortunately for my sanity, Angel took control and eventually I was able to string together a coherent sentence and a business transaction involving him agreeing to come back and buy some ferrets from me ensued.

He was actually quite a nice chap. We became friends of sorts and I often wondered why I'd dreamt about him? What was the meaning of the dream? Was something meant to happen between us? I was really into Mr Man at the time and he was also with someone. Devil kept telling me to shag him of course, no surprises there, but we didn't and it felt OK that we didn't. Years later I'm still none the wiser what any of that was all about.

The next time I experienced this I'm going to blame Jason Statham. I watch a few of his films and really like them but he doesn't float my boat at all. Then along comes The Transporter. I watch it, love it and watch it several more times. He's not my type as such but there's something about him in this particular film. I begin having a recurring dream about a guy who looks similar but not identical. I'm working on a shoot at the time so everyone dresses in green and there's always a meeting around the big gun cleaning table in the bothy, to discuss tactics for the day's shooting in the morning, and later in the day for gun cleaning duties. I never stay for the gun cleaning as I'm not a loader so it's not my job but I often overhear bits of the chat and banter as I'm leaving. It's usually sex or gossip related, I guess to make a boring, banal task more enjoyable.

I begin having a recurring dream about this Statham looky-likey sitting opposite me around the table. He never talks or smiles, he just sits there in his green shooting jumper staring back at me. I have the dream so many times I get rid of the transporter DVD to make sure I don't watch it and keep this loop going, but every now and then there he is. He keeps popping up. It doesn't feel like another Deja Reve like the guy before as he looks familiar, but it niggles at me until one night I actually chase after him as the meeting ends to try to talk to him. I feel like I'm on the verge of lucid dreaming as my plan is to corner him and ask why he's there in my dream. He ignores me and jumps into a green Land Rover and drives off across the moors, leaving me standing feeling puzzled and stupid in equal measures.

This is also the moment I realise I'm dreaming as the track from the Head Gamekeepers moor is different to the track he drives along and this breaks the spell. I realise I've lost control of the dream as I'm on foot standing there like a divvy. A proper lucid dreamer would just jump in the air and fly after him, hovering in front shouting "Why you invading my dream-space Jase?" through the power of telepathic thought. Eventually the dreams subside and I make a point of not watching any more Statham movies to try to give him the dream world cold shoulder which eventually works.

Until up pops Mr Irishman with the dog.

Devil is telling me "this is your dream guy, literally. You have to meet him. It's destiny. Your next great fuck is just around the corner" (and across the sea)

Angel is saying "OK, he has a green jumper and is bald but other than that I just don't get it? Be careful you're not trying to shove a round peg into a square hole. Besides, aren't you sick of men by now? Shouldn't you really be getting help? It's not normal to be this obsessed with sex".

Devil tells her to shut up and get off my case, everyone's secretly obsessed with sex, the human race would be in a sorry state if we all suddenly became androgynous dullards who no longer wanted to procreate. Even if I'm not strictly procreating, I'm practising, which is the next best thing.

See if you can guess who I should have listened to, and who I actually listened to in a future chapter. I think you know the answer by now.

Chapter 14

Hard Work

Spoiler Alert :

If you enjoy drinking milk don't read this chapter! If you did enjoy drinking it and now don't as a result of reading ahead anyway.......Sorry but you were warned! This chapter also contains graphic descriptions of sexual fantasies. If you're OK with that, please keep reading.

I've had some truly grotty and tedious jobs over the years, some of them preferable to being unemployed and on the constant carousel of trying and failing to find the perfect job, others much less so. I've cleaned workmen's portacabins where it looked like they had a food fight with jam, coffee and coleslaw. I've attempted to unblock toilets where people have kept shitting on top of other people's shit until the toilet resembles a giant anthill of poo. You can't by the way, unblock it I mean. Just don't go there.

One of the worst jobs I had was when I worked on a so-called charity farm run by a pair of

eccentric butch women, one definitely bordering more on egocentric than eccentric.

When I say charity they were in the process of trying to become one but mainly they just used volunteer workers, many of them migrants, to perform all the animal care duties for their menagerie that they couldn't be bothered to do themselves. Plus the biggest, craziest one got off on the power trip of bossing people around. Due to her awful disposition and the fact the migrant workers were offered a cold, dingy caravan as living quarters, they had a high turnover of staff. I had been out of work for some time and as "working with animals" was number one on my list of job requirements, I was drawn to the idea of working there in the beginning. There was a government scheme going whereby they paid a large sum of money direct to the big bad butches, who then paid me a weekly wage for looking after the animals. It sounded like a fair cop to me and the other girls who worked there regularly seemed nice.

It wasn't long before I sussed out what was really going on. I saw several staff come and go, all equally disgruntled at the way they were treated, mostly in tears, young men and women alike she would reduce them to floods. The lists of jobs became endless and the big bad boss's behaviour became more and more aggressive and erratic as the weeks went on. I quickly realised she got off on being horrible to people and getting as much work out of them as possible for as little money. The minute I saw her for what she really was I decided three things. Number one none of that shit would wash with me she was not getting to keep the money, that was my money and I was damn well staying put until I'd been given every penny owed to me. Number two she was not going to treat me like a human doormat or ever reduce me to tears like she did everyone else. Finally number three I was going to do the bare minimum work possible to get by each day until the job contract ended.

This didn't go down well as she liked to have you doing all sorts of random things like picking up every tiny bit of straw from in between the gravel in the yard on your hands and knees. I think if she could have gotten away with it she would have made us scrub toilets with toothbrushes or cut the grass lawn with scissors. She began writing in a book all the things we were not doing, or not doing to her satisfaction and every morning we would either have to read her ever more insane rants or listen as she came to shout the same things at us as were written in the "Bad Book"

I made a point of just staring at her the whole time not reacting to her outbursts, then just going about my business as though she hadn't said anything at all which I think really pissed her off! She wanted me to either protest or kick back so she could have an argument and a reason to sack me, or to cry cos she had a fetish about watching hot girls blubbing their eyes out. I gave her nothing and it really annoyed her. The rants in the book got angrier and angrier, sometimes the pages were torn she had scribbled them so fervently. I should have felt pity for her as it reminded me of my angry diary I had as a child, but nope. When none of this got the desired reaction she took to writing all over the walls in black magic marker. I literally couldn't wait to get out of there and had my last payment and leaving date circled on the calendar. If only I'd had the same wisdom and foresight to treat the man who came into my life next with the same boundaries I would have less chapters to write but that's hindsight for you!

One evening after a particularly awful day doing menial tasks and watching her verbally assault people, I spotted a post on social media where a few friends were discussing a documentary they'd seen the night before. It was about women who made a fortune in the sex chat line industry. Back then it was big business, there weren't the copious amounts of free porn that today's internet has to offer. Men had to pay to have an orgasm if they couldn't find a woman to have one with. My ears were pricked up so I watched it instantly thinking to myself well I could do that! I'm pretty sure I might be better at it than some of the ladies on the program too. At that time I wasn't getting any anyway. I was more than a bit fed up with men, most of them seemed to be ignorant turds, no good in bed, or both so I was just focussed on trying to get by. If this was a way to make extra money whilst exploiting the hell out of pervert men, well sign me up!

A few discreet enquiries later to find the company with the best rates and I was all set to go. I listened to some of the other women's messages who worked for the company first as research to make sure I had something which stood out from the crowd. A lot of them sounded old, grumpy and not enthusiastic about what they were selling. I recorded a message which sounded light, giggly, suggestive and sat back and waited for the calls to come in.

It turns out men don't just want mucky women to make them come, yes some do but also lots don't. Some men just want someone nice they can have a sexy chat with to fulfil their fantasies. Some were disabled and some were widowers who missed female company, they were a wide cross section of all ages from all over the UK. I decided to be the best I needed to be to beat the rest so grabbing my trusty essentials, a noisy vibrator, a cup of water and a notepad and pen, I set out to make as many men come as I could. Watching the pennies from the penises turn in to pounds and the zeros on the bank balance grow was more satisfying than actual sex, at least in those early stages.

The cup of water came in handy so many times. It turns out a lot of men want to hear a woman go to the toilet and fantasise she's using their body as a loo, weird I know but they were willing to pay for it so I would make sure and take my sweet time pouring that cup down the pan, to the accompaniment of satisfied noises.

Only once did a guy want me to do a jobby on him and I didn't have a prop to simulate the plop so I just had to improvise with suitable pushing sounds. The noisy vibrator, that's self-explanatory and the notepad and paper well... that was probably most important of all because on that I would jot down the guy's name, any significant details he mentioned about himself and in a few words what his fetish and trigger words were. I would use different phrases during our chats and listen closely for the ones that seemed to tip him over the edge and make sure not to use them until the very last so I would earn more money. The quicker he pops his load the less pennies you get, so you want to satisfy him but not too fast. It also strokes their ego to hear you go "Oh Hi Barry! I've been so hoping you would call big boy, we had such fun last time" That's what keeps them coming back, thinking that you actually did have an orgasm whilst talking to him on the phone, even if inside you are actually crying with laughter.

There are rules to the job, not many but you aren't allowed to talk about anything under 16, rightly so! And you aren't allowed to hang up the call, the caller must always end it. This didn't

present a problem to begin with as I seemed to
get very few callers who wanted to pretend I
was an underage girl and when I did I would
just firmly say No I am not willing to discuss
that it is illegal you do know that don't you?
These callers always made my guts churn with
disgust. Half of me wanted to reach down the
phone and strangle them for being a pedo, the
other half thought well, what if talking to me
stops them from harming a child? It was a
quandary I could never settle in my mind,
Number one was always the most appealing
option.

I'd been doing the job for a few weeks when my
final day at the farm came, I was so happy! I
wasn't earning enough yet from the sex work to
do that full time, plus who would want to? It's
pretty intense! I'd been offered a seasonal job
on a shoot and also some work for a local
agricultural company, both working outdoors
which I love best so I was happy to juggle the
three part time jobs rather than commit to one
full time one, plus the sex work was best for
evenings anyway.

On my last day big crazy boss came up to me
grovelling, asking me to stay as I was the "Best

worker they had ever had" She even gave me a big card gushing about how great I was and a small gift as an incentive, but I was determined now I'd earned all of the grant and they hadn't had a penny I was outta there. I bet she still has sick fantasies to this day about making me cry, she did try so hard to make it happen.

I had a new career as a sex chat girl to focus on and whilst in retrospect I'm not the proudest of this part of my life, I did have some amazing belly laughs with my friends about some of the weirdos and what they wanted to do to me, or me to do to them. Or what they wanted the milking machine to do to them in the case of one particularly strange chap who rang me one evening.

I used to quite enjoy my milky Weetabix and ever since this chat I've never been able to look at the white stuff without feeling like I'm going to barf, so if you enjoy milk you might want to look away for the next couple of paragraphs.

Three hours I had to endure, yes three! Of this actually very nice and at first normal sounding dairy farmer from Ayrshire. It began with some strange stuff right off the bat and I quickly knew this was going to be a call that would stick in my mind forever. He told me he liked to put the cow's milking machine on his cock at the end of the day after he had milked them all, before he cleaned the equipment. Inside I was throwing up, but I kept a straight face and indulged him by pushing it a step further, what if he just came into the milk and people got to drink it including me? He loved that I was joining in instead of the repulsive reaction I was actually feeling inside. He excitedly said he'd actually already done this lots of times and it was so good to have someone to talk to about it. His fantasies then went on to become progressively more bizarre ones involving the milking machine sucking his dick right off his body, cutting off his own penis and feeding it to people or being staked out on the beach naked and watching crabs come up and nibble at him while he was still alive, starting of course with yes, you guessed it, his dick. How I endured that three hour ordeal without bursting into laughter and calling him a sicko I do not know but what I do know is I've never drunk milk again since just incase! If there's ever a headline in the Scottish news saying dairy farmer found dead with penis sucked off by milking machine, I will not be the least bit surprised!

I'd been doing the sex chat girl thing for a while when Mr Irishman popped up on an internet forum I was on and after chatting backwards and forwards for a few weeks we met up for breakfast. We played it down, as if it was just two doggy friends meeting up for a quick chat, but really it was our first date. It was an odd one really looking back. There were red flags from that first meeting but I chose to ignore them, stupid me!

He seemed very nervous and fidgety, glued to his phone which I found quite ignorant when you're trying to have a conversation with someone, plus he was balder and less attractive than his photos and had freckles. Angel is saying "walk away this is not the guy for you" Devil is saying "when was the last time you saw an actual real, live man's penis apart from the plastic one you pretend to play with every night to make money"?

Devil you bane of my life you!

I don't tell Mr Irishman straight away about all of my jobs, only the respectable two but in our very many and very lengthy chats that have become a daily thing, he wants to know everything there is to know about me and seems to think I'm wonderful, so I cautiously say I have a third job but don't immediately tell him what it is. A girl has to have some mystery after all. He tells me he works in a hospital and is also a part time fireman, one night a week, which almost seven years later I find out was total bullshit, he was actually doing Chinese takeaway deliveries but eventually after many wrong guesses, I tell him about my secret wee side-line.

He loves it, he thinks it's great, he already seems to hang on my every word so this is the cherry on top. Free sexy chats right? No, I quickly tell him I don't mix business with pleasure and he manages to hide his disappointment fairly well. He seems like a really sound guy, so into me and taking everything in his stride, I begin to think maybe he has potential?

We talk late into the night when I'm not working the chat lines and he sends me good morning and good night messages every day. He's so attentive even though we're not yet in a relationship it almost feels like we are. We meet up again, not for very long as he's over from Ireland on business and doesn't have much time. Another red flag pops up when he says he can't take me out to dinner as originally planned, could I come and meet him instead as he's running late for his ferry. Angel tells me firmly "No, don't do it, if you go running now he will think you're desperate and you'll always be running after him". I say I'm disappointed as I thought we were going on a proper date but he somehow manages to beg and plead with me to come see him as if I don't it will be a few weeks before we can meet again properly. I relent and go which was a huge mistake but at the time it doesn't feel like one. We chat for a while and he tells me how smitten he is with me and we share a kiss goodbye. Angel says "maybe he's a decent guy, give him a chance then, better him than some other creepy walking hard-on" and I'm sold. We begin a long distance relationship where he is super attentive and doting in the times in between visits. Those first six months or so feel like a whirlwind where I'm swept off my feet with compliments and promises of a great future ahead 'til my head is swirling with it all. This is what true love feels like right?

I never knew about love bombing or future faking until it was much too late. I know a lot about them now though.

I have to be honest, I was very naïve and although I did spot red flags I was able to dismiss them as being me "Just being silly" after all we had lots in common and he seemed so attentive, the most attentive any man has been towards me ever. I had also never heard of the word narcissist, because if I had I might have recognised the signs, the way markers along the slippery slope I was travelling. He had all the classic con man's traits, using my name a lot, most likely so he could remember it amongst all the other women he was secretly wooing in tandem with me, hanging off my every word, wanting to know my thoughts and opinions on everything and of course trying to fast forward to our future, speeding up the process of getting to know one another carnally as well as normally.

Something that niggled me was when he would say things like "When you get to our age" as though I should just hop straight into bed with him because my forties were fast approaching. He said he respected me taking my time and being cautious due to the distance involved in our potentially budding relationship, but at the same time he wanted to constantly remind me that I wasn't getting any younger. A few times I

felt like saying "speak for yourself Mister! I'm
not quite ready for the scrap heap just yet" but
really what was happening was he was
constantly testing my boundaries.
Simultaneously trying to figure out where all my
weak spots were so he could use them against
me at a later date. All the late night chats were
just a way of sussing out how "easy" I was
going to be to build up then break down.

Narcissists love to do this; it's all a big game to
them. The aim of the game is to make you feel
special and who doesn't when a guy tells you
constantly how wonderful you are, how he's
never met anyone quite like you before and how
much he admires and respects you as well as
fancies your pants off. I'm being honest here it
did appeal to my ego, he stroked it so hard I did
start to feel like I was floating up there on a
cloud. That's phase one of the Narcissist Master
Plan, put you up there on a pedestal as high as
they can possibly place you. Phase two comes
later. they begin to pick away at your character,
looks, core values and vulnerabilities, taking one
piece away at a time until you either say
enough's enough and get out or you come
tumbling down.

I knew none of this and just went along for the ride thinking well I had been infatuated with Mr Man but maybe this was what true love was meant to feel like? Maybe I wasn't supposed to instantly feel that crotch tingling attraction and urge to rip his clothes off I'd had with Mr Man? He didn't love me so I needed to stop basing all my other interactions with men on him. He was a tall order to match up to. Maybe true love was meant to grow slowly? Was it meant to be a flickering flame that would eventually become a raging fire?

A few dates later we decided we knew each other well enough to hit the bedroom. It was after a really pleasant date where he was an old fashioned gent pulling out the chair for me and listening intently to everything I had to say no matter how banal. I thought well what's the worst that can happen if he's a crap shag maybe we can work on it? If he's a good one then that's a bonus. I think my ovaries were talking to me that night saying "Settle down with Mr Nice, haven't you had enough of the bad boys?" so off to bed we went.

It was disappointing to say the least. His cock was smaller than he had described it to be and

the minute I saw it I wanted to just toss him off
and get it over with so I could go home and
reflect on whether or not this was a good match
for me. He wanted me to put it in my mouth and
I made the excuse that I didn't like that. A lie of
course, because If I do like a guy and I'm really
into him then it just comes naturally. He begs
and pleads with me just lick the tip, I give it a
try and he has this horrible slimy cock which
doesn't taste good at all. I make my excuses
and say sorry I'm really not into that. He seems
pretty upset, we have sex instead and its equally
disappointing, first times are rarely earth
shattering, it usually takes a few attempts to get
comfortable with each other's bodies but this
feels like one of the most boring shags I've ever
had. Lying next to him afterwards feels all
wrong too so I make a very poor excuse and cut
the night short so I can head home. He doesn't
handle this well and bombards me with more
messages and compliments than ever before. He
tells me he was just so overcome with nerves
about sleeping with me for the first time
because I mean so much to him but promises it
will get better.

Against my better judgement I agree to see him
again.

Chapter 15

Happy Couples?

Fast forward a few months and I'm now in a long distance relationship with The Irishman. I've never been in one before and have a lot of reservations about it. General consensus seems to be they are very hard things to make work. I do worry quite a lot about the chemistry side of things too. He doesn't give me fanny flutters like Mr Man did, things take much longer to get going but I get around this by telling myself that I've never had a relationship like this before. Only a large helping of casual sex with guys I couldn't give two hoots about, a handful of relationships where the guys were more into me than I was them. I had no issues getting shot of them and then there was Mr Man who I would have walked across hot coals for but he didn't feel the same way. I kept telling myself I'd never really experienced "True Love" maybe this was the way it was meant to feel? The sex is getting slightly better although I still don't want to put it anywhere near my mouth. He has this horrible, off-putting, droopy foreskin it looks like something that fell out of a kangaroo's pouch.

We do get along well together though when he's here, we share the same hobbies and interests and he seems to be besotted with me. When were apart he's super attentive sending me love notes and is incapable of passing a card or gift shop without sending me something nice. He calls me his "Princess" "Precious" and "Angle" and his awful spelling does grate on me, but I try to look past that to the sentiment behind it. He seems to be the perfect guy on paper at least. He tells me he was in a 16 year relationship with a woman but it ended about 6 months ago. The reason they split, he tells me, is because she had severe depression and their sex life dwindled until it was non-existent. They lived together but didn't share a bed for a long time. He has a teenage daughter with her and stayed so long so he could be a good dad to her which seems legit, or maybe I just wanted it to be so? He currently lives with his elderly mother back in his old childhood bedroom and works 4 days a week in a hospital and one night a week in a fire station. He loves coming over here and ideally wants to move here. All sounding fairly promising so far.

He does keep pushing for sexy chats in between our visits, obviously as this is one of my part time jobs he thinks he's entitled to the same treatment for free. But somehow it just doesn't feel right to me. I feel like I can chat freely with the strangers who are paying me to as I'll never meet them in person. This feels different, if he's my Mr Right I'm not sure I want to be full on filthy in case it puts him off. He reassures me nothing I say or do will put him off, he's madly in love with me and has been since the first morning we met in the café. I'm taken aback as it all seems very fast, but I get swept along for the ride as he constantly bombards me with messages and phone calls about how I'm the perfect woman, he's never met anyone he's so into before.

I relent and send him a few sexy stories to listen to while he's at work. He likes to go into the hospital toilets and wank off to them. I think Ok, fair enough he has a point when he keeps saying we need to keep things spicy as there's that distance involved. When I say we, he really means I need to, because as he keeps telling me that if I don't then the relationship won't work. I naively don't recognise these early signs of him trying to dominate the relationship with his needs, I just think well at least he's being honest with me like I am with him and perhaps I should make more of an effort to please him. He also likes to video call me from his room at home and I say dirty stuff to him while he wanks. I still don't feel comfortable with any of this as I have to pretend that I'm also really horny and masturbating, I have to make videos of myself and play on screen while he is. It should feel natural and just flow, but for some reason it doesn't? If I've learned anything from what was to happen in the years that followed it's that your gut is telling you things for a reason, you need to listen to it, even if you can't immediately put your finger on what's wrong.

His elderly Mother is in the early stages of dementia and sometimes she comes into the room while he's jerking off. I find this really disturbing and tell him he should fit a lock to his door. He doesn't seem to care, he gets off on the whole thrill seeking thing of almost getting caught, both by danger wanking in the toilets at work and at home. This doesn't sit right with me but I feel obliged to continue the charade now as it's become the main way I keep him entertained during the waiting period in between visits. It keeps niggling at me that I don't feel wild horny or a willing participant the way I would have if it had been Mr Man. He was dyslexic and couldn't even send text messages never mind work a mobile phone or computer so we never engaged in any sort of cybersex, only ever the real thing.

He keeps asking me about my work and if I enjoy it and I admit that I'm beginning to tire of it as one of the girls who must have been handling all the worst pervert calls has left and I'm now getting them!

They start off talking about the usual stuff, then they try to push the boundaries of what's allowed. Sex chat line rules are anything goes as long as it's not illegal. Several men call me every time I'm working a shift and this is all they want to talk about. It makes me sick to my stomach as well as angry. It grates against my conscience as I feel like I'm facilitating these creeps by even talking to them, but the no hang up rule means I just have to say over and over that I am 16 and I can't discuss anything illegal with them. One guy keeps calling and eventually gets really pissed off with me and says "Well Jennifer used to let me talk about anything I wanted to" to which I lose the plot and say "Well go and call Jennifer then you fucking pedo"! It feels so good to finally say what I'm really feeling but I then begin to worry if I'll get caught out. The company can listen in to any calls at any time so if I'm found out I'll be sacked. I wrestle back and forth with whether or not I want to carry on with this. I wish I could get their numbers in some way so I could report them, but it's all done through a private server so I have no way of tracing them. The company doesn't seem to really care as they don't have any reporting procedure in place. I can't make this work in my mind, it feels like my job which was once a laugh and a giggle, has now become a seedy and immoral way to earn money.

I share this with Mr Irishman, he always wants to know everything about how I'm feeling, what I'm doing and everything about me. Another red flag I failed to notice. It's good to take an interest in your partner but interest can quickly become obsession. Things come to a head one day I'm working on my farming job and I receive a distressed call from a neighbour that there's a burst pipe in my house and the water is pouring into my elderly next door neighbour's house through her walls and ceiling. Could I please come home immediately? I'm in the middle of nowhere in a muddy cow field so the answer's no. She rings me back to tell me the police are here, they're going to boot the door in and there's an emergency plumber here to sort out whatever the problem is. I'm not best happy about this but there's little I can do about it so I tell them to do whatever they need to do to fix it. It turns out to be a problem with one of the radiator valves and is quickly sorted. However, I'd been working the chat lines the night before and left my work gear on the bed when I left to go to my day job. An assortment of large noisy dildos and a clipboard containing scores and scores of men's names with their filthy kinks written alongside them. Next to each one I would write the duration of the call, so I could identify the biggest earners and devote most of my energy into keeping them coming back for more.

I cringe inwardly as I realise the policemen and plumber might see this. I can't remember if I closed the bedroom door over when I left. I don't think I did? It might be one of the first things they see as the bedroom is right there as you enter the house. Also, my neighbour didn't say where the water was coming through so if it's the bedroom I'm screwed. I chuckle and cringe in equal measures, it's one of those situations you have to laugh really, there's simply nothing else for it.

I return from a long shift to find the bedroom door as I suspected wide open, the dildos on the bed look as though they may have been picked up and inspected and worst of all the clipboard which had been lying open is closed over. They are either really bad at hiding the fact they have snooped through my sordid stuff, or they have done it on purpose to let me know that they did. I'm not sure which one is worse really. I do find it funny as well as cringeworthy and end up telling a couple of my female friends who think it's hilarious. They always enjoy hearing about my antics anyway, one of them even says I should write a book about my sexploits, and here we are.

My phone pings and it's two friend requests from two guys I've never heard of, no mutual friends. I snoop their profiles and both are young guys, I only need to look at their occupation to realise these are the plumbers who attended today. I quickly block and delete both of them and think what a pair of pervy chancers. Mind you, the things that were written in my work folder probably made them think they were in with a good chance.

When Mr Irishman calls me that evening I tell him about the day's events giggling away as I do, expecting him to see the funny side of things but he reacts in quite the opposite way. He's fuming, I've never heard him angry like this before, he goes off on a rant about how he didn't want to say before, but now that were in a serious relationship he doesn't want "his" girl doing such a shady job. It's disgusting that the plumbers would try to make contact with me. I should report them! I say I've deleted them and I don't want to cause a fuss. He says he wants me to give the job up, I'm not happy about the underage thing anyway so now this has happened I should stop. He would rather give me part of his wage than see me carry on doing such a vile job. I don't want his wage, I'm perfectly capable of finding myself another job. He's been a real old fashioned gent up until now paying for everything and refusing to let me lift a finger, but being financially supported by a man is something I could never be comfortable with. I watched my Mum tied like this to my Dad so I'd always said I would never get into a situation where I was dependent on a man for anything, least of all money. I agree I'm going to quit the job after I finish out this week's agreed shifts.

I think that's the end of the rant and my decision will bring things to a close but no, he's just getting warmed up. He now begins to turn things on me asking why did I leave all the stuff lying on the bed for anyone to find? Why was I laughing about it, did I find it funny? Wasn't I ashamed? I defend myself by saying I lock my door when I leave the house and hadn't exactly expected a bunch of workmen to go traipsing through my stuff. I found it funny because it was funny really once you put aside the initial embarrassment and no I didn't feel ashamed, just a bit cringey which the laughter helped with. He then proceeded to tell me he thought I should be disgusted and then made some nasty comments about me previously having an affair with Mr Man. I was shocked as I didn't really see the connection to today's events. I had disclosed that we had an affair when we first met and he didn't seem to have an issue with it, he said he appreciated my honesty and that he had made a lot of mistakes in his life too. This was the first time he was to use my past as a verbal stick to beat me with. The first of so, so many. If I could have seen into the future then just how many times, I would have ended things right there and hung up the phone on him for good.

So that was our first argument. It felt horrible. Things had been so nice up until then, he thought I was amazing, intelligent, beautiful, funny, kind, caring, awesome, amazing, every complimentary word you can think of and more. Now he was upset with me, disappointed, disgusted. Perhaps I wasn't the girl for him after all? He had expected me to handle the situation a certain way and I had done the opposite so now I was out of his favour.

It felt awful over the next few days as he was colder in his messages and calls, they were much shorter and I felt a distance growing between us.

Of course this was just the façade slipping and I was getting to see the "real" him for the first time. A deception can only be kept going for so long and eventually the mask will start to drop. I should have been seeing this as a red flag for me to also pull back and say, "well if you don't like it, tough. I can't change my past, I'm quitting the job anyway, and it's not as though

I'm going to run off with the plumber so dry your eyes and move on".

Instead I fall headfirst into his trap.

I started trying to win his good favour back and the moment I did this, he was able to really begin playing his narcissistic mind games as this was my first test. I'd passed with flying colours, proving I was a suitable candidate for emotional manipulation. I asked if he was OK? This is the worst thing you can ever ask a narcissist because it opens up the door for them to begin to berate you with everything that's not OK in their horrible world. They begin to project all of their insecurities and issues onto you by nit picking at yours until you feel you're going mad. The first stage of his plan which was to love bomb me onto a pedestal was complete, now phase two began where he'd play emotional Jenga with me, slowly pulling one brick at a time out of my defensive walls until he could crash through and reduce me to a crumbled, messy pile.

Over the next 6 years he would regularly bring up things to brow beat me with. Why was I friends on Facebook with so and so? Had I slept with him? How many men had I slept with? I managed to dodge this question for a while but he kept telling me he found it disgusting that I had an affair with a man 20 years older than me. In his eyes any woman who has had more than 5 sexual partners in her life before meeting him was a slut and not marriage material. So I had to lie and say less than 5. I don't to this day know why I did. I should have just had some balls and said "I've slept with quite a few men, more than some women, much less than others, but I can't control my past so you either accept me as I am or bugger off!" I contemplated the words a few times when he was raving about something or other, since this initial argument the rantings and ravings became more and more regular. I don't know why, but the more he tried to run me down the harder I would try to adjust things to keep him happy. What a waste of time and energy that turned out to be!

It didn't matter how many male friends I deleted from social media or stopped chatting to, or how much I swore blind I didn't still have a torch for Mr Man or any of the other things he accused me of, nothing was ever going to get me back up on the pedestal again. I was now somehow soiled, lesser, not worthy in his mind. He was having serious doubts about the type of woman I was and if he would ever be able to have a proper, serious relationship with me. I became so busy trying to be the perfect girlfriend I failed to go "Whoah Mister, who says I am decided that you are the right guy for ME from your recent behaviour?"

To add stress to an already stressful situation, all of this was going on during a period where we were apart. Although we had a date coming up where we would be able to see each other for a day or two, he was now dangling that meeting in front of me like some sort of prize, making me feel that if things weren't fully sorted out by that time maybe he wouldn't come over after all.

You might be thinking to yourself reading this why the hell didn't I just tell him to sod off? I honestly don't know. It's something I'm working on figuring out as I type. The conclusion I've come to so far is that because of my troubled childhood I tend to be drawn more towards abusive relationships, even though that's the furthest thing from what I really want. Also that there's something inherently lacking in me, some kind of deep rooted need for praise, acceptance and love that made me strive to please him more instead of looking after number one. The same flaw which made me a slave to my cruel friend's mind games as a child. Once I formed a close bond with someone, I would endure all sorts of horrendous treatment out of a misguided sense of loyalty to them. Because those bread crumbs of praise they sparingly dished out would remind me of nicer times, when the friendship or relationship was just forming and the praise was given lavishly.

When we finally met up we had such a lovely romantic day it was like something out of a fairy-tale and I genuinely didn't want it to end. I did manage to pluck up my courage though and speak up about how he had treated me. We went for a walk along the beach and later, sitting on the rocks watching the waves roll in and out, I told him I wanted to open up about how I felt. He seemed very attentive and wanted to hear what I had to say.

I told him we were getting along well, but the argument had really thrown me and I was upset he had used my past as something to throw at me during it. I told him I wasn't proud of the affair I'd had and it was a mistake I didn't ever intend to repeat. I didn't think it was fair of him to bring it up and I wanted him to promise not to do it again. The past was the past and couldn't be changed so let's focus on the future. He agreed to that and said he just couldn't bear the thought of me with any other man apart from him and we kissed and made up. I thought that was the end of it all and breathed a sigh of relief and began looking hopefully forward to getting back on track.

In reality what I'd really done was not make peace but kindle war, I'd handed him my weakest spot on a plate, he now knew what would hurt and upset me for future arguments. It was safely stored away in his evil blackmail bank for future use. In the meantime though, he got swiftly back to work on building me back up on the pedestal telling me how wonderful I was, despite the fact I was soiled by other men. He was big enough to look past that and forgive me. He didn't like women who slept with other men before him, but he would make an exception for me 'cos he loved me so much. There the cycle began, just as the sea washes up against the rocks and batters against their rough edges until they become rounded off, he was about to embark on a campaign of building me up and then knocking me down until eventually he could dispense with the building up process and just knock me down, further and further down, until I was his personal doormat.

Chapter 16

Hospital

It's the day of my operation today and I'm a nervous wreck! For several years now I've had tumours growing inside me until they reached the point where I look 6 months pregnant. Thankfully they are uterine fibroids and not cancerous, but a scan reveals they have been steadily growing in there for years and have started to turn calcified. I've had a course of painful injections over the last 6 months in an attempt to shrink the tumours down to facilitate surgery and a total hysterectomy is now the best solution.

If only I'd had the sense to have a man-ectomy beforehand and rid myself of the parasitic, passive-aggressive and abusive relationship I had been in for the last 6 years. Things went steadily downhill from that day at the beach. He began playing mind games all the time, there didn't seem to be any break from them. If it wasn't one game it was another. One of his favourites was to tell me about girls who were messaging him. I dubbed this one the "rub my nose in it" game. I'd be at home minding my own business and he would send a photo of some girl. It got to the point I would dread opening up my phone, I would leave it as long as I possibly could without also activating the "Where are you? What are you doing?" game, another favourite. That one involved me saying what I was doing, making it sound as boring as possible and him replying with lots more questions as though he didn't believe me. Sometimes I would send a photo of where I was or what I was doing to bring the game to a halt. It didn't always work but a lot of the time I genuinely was doing boring stuff so it would satisfy his urge to make sure I wasn't fitting in some secret sex with some other guy. After all as he loved to remind me, I used to have secret sex with someone else's husband, Didn't I? Such a dirty girl, Didn't I feel ashamed?

Anyway, back to the girl games. It began as a seemingly innocent thing one day he cautiously said to me that some random girl had messaged him on social media trying to chat him up and get him to go out for a drink with her. He said he just wanted to be totally honest and transparent with me, because he was into me and me only, but he couldn't control the fact that there were all these wild women out there flinging themselves at him. England, Scotland, Wales, Ireland, you name it. He was apparently this irresistible woman magnet, I should really feel so lucky that he had chosen me!

The girl was stunning of course. I was miffed but found it hard to show my annoyance because he went on to say that he was really breaking "guy code" by telling me about this. He reckoned 90% of men get this bombardment of women wanting to have sex with them on a regular basis. Even the ugly men, which I found a hard one to believe? But he assured me oh yes, women are filthy these days and I was actually very old fashioned, prudish and frigid by comparison. Frigid was a word I had grown to loathe. The first time he called me that I was shocked. Calling a former sex worker frigid. What glitch in the Matrix made that happen? I was hearing it more and more these days. I was old, dull, frumpy and frigid, and these girls were new and exciting. They would message whether you were single or not. If they liked what they saw they just had to have you. If you said no you had a girlfriend or wife, this made a lot of women even more determined.

He was telling me because he was proud of the fact he was different to every other man I'd ever met, so he was going to tell me and show me, not to upset me of course, purely to be honest and transparent about everything that was happening.

So I had two choices, one was end it so he could go off and explore all these new avenues, the other was to just sort of suck it up and get on with it, because the way he worded it was he wanted there to be complete trust between us. If I happened to see some girl on his phone it would just be one of these crazed psycho-sluts and I was to immediately discount it. I wasn't happy with this and argued that there shouldn't be any conversations with women, surely all that's needed is for him to say sorry I've got a girlfriend I'm not interested and then block or delete if they persist? I reason with him that that's what I would do if some random man messaged me, or I might even just block and delete without even replying. I think this is a perfectly reasonable request but that then gives him the angle to start quizzing me to see if I'm getting men messaging me. Classic narcissist, deflect the topic onto the other person and then turn it all around and blame them!

The fact of the matter is I'm run down emotionally and mentally, my health's not the best, I feel stressed all the time, I certainly don't look or feel attractive. I'm probably the last woman a horny man would want to message right now. Maybe if there had been a man or two messaging me it might have let me know I had options instead of sticking doggedly to this one, who was on a mission to completely deplete and ruin my self-confidence.

We argue back and forth about it and he eventually concedes that I'm right, if any more women message him he will just do exactly as I've suggested. It's a relief to have the subject brought to a close, but so annoying I should even have to tell him how he should behave when women proposition him. Surely a caring man would just deal with it quietly and discreetly and not need to rub his girlfriend's face in it all? The most recent one is a pretty red head who has apparently just messaged him out of the blue asking him if he wants to go and spend the weekend at her lovely barn conversion in Cheshire. She'd love to do a threesome with him and her female friend. He's not showing me this of course to upset me or make me jealous, no he's only showing me to be totally honest, open and transparent. So I can be really proud of my man who's not like other men. Other men he assures me would only ever do one of two things. They would shag the women behind my back and I'd never know. Or they would knock them back and not tell me. Either way I wouldn't be in the loop. He's keeping me in the loop cos he's Mr Super Honest and I should feel really lucky and privileged to be with such a rare species.

All the other men out there are untrustworthy turds, dipping their wicks left, right and centre but no not him, he's a real catch and I should feel honoured to have such a man in my life. I try to argue that not every man is like that, my brother Lloyd has been happily married for many years, not all guys are cheats. He laughs and says I'm naïve if I think anyone is happily married. He tells me his friend's been having an affair with his wives best friend, she's found out and is devastated. I'm shocked to hear this, his friend seems a really genuine family man, surely not? He tells me it's true. I say well in that case she is better off without both him and her so called friend, with a friend like that who needs enemies?

He tells me she is a "real woman" because she's going to take him back. Real women take men back who make mistakes. He watches me closely to see my reaction and I say no thanks, if he cheated on me he is out. I've said that from day one, that's one of my major deal breakers. He tells me he would take me back if I cheated on him. He looks at me as though he's waiting for me to confess something? There's nothing to say as I've not so much looked at another man the whole time we've been together, let alone strayed so I say well that's irrelevant, one I wouldn't cheat and two if I did I wouldn't deserve to be taken back. He goes quiet, I don't realise it at the time, but he's actually cheating on me behind my back and is testing the water to see what my reaction would be if I found out. It's probably easier to keep attacking me in subtle ways to wear me down so he can eventually let the cat out of the bag, I'll be so broken by then I won't end things. He has work to do to break my spirit fully.

I should also try harder to be slimmer and better looking, I've let myself go a lot lately, look how chubby I'm getting. I'm not keeping things spicy enough in the bedroom. I should join a gym. He goes to the gym and trains 6 days a week. He only does this so he can look good for me, nobody else, so really I'm being very lazy and selfish by not being slim, toned and athletic for him. Of course if I did join a gym I'd have to make sure I don't be too obvious about anything I'm doing while I'm there for fear I might catch other guy's eyes. There are women out there who dress in skimpy outfits and go to the gym just to come on to men. He knows this cos women come on to him at the gym all the time. He makes sure to tell me about each and every one of them and their wily ways. I bet Miss Redhead goes to the gym, just look at her figure. He's never had a threesome, it might be quite nice to have one. Obviously not with the red head who just offered him one of course, but maybe if I could make more of an effort to be the ultimate girlfriend, he might want to have one with me and another girl maybe? If I was up for that? But there's so much work to do first, I'm so fat and lazy and don't make an effort anymore. We have such a long way to go to get there because I've been so soiled by other men, it's going to take time to turn me into a worthy girlfriend.

Somewhere amongst this madness I decide the best thing to do is ask him to please not send me any more photos of the girls that want to have orgies with him. It seems much easier since he is so open, honest and transparent, just to let him handle it quietly by letting them know he's taken. Am I sure he asks? I just want to be open and honest at all times? I say yes, I don't want to see or hear about it anymore.

I've never been a "Pick me" type of girl, if a man tries to make me compare or compete with other women I prefer to walk away, but in hindsight this was his way of trying to drum me down so low in confidence that I would either begin to really go all out to win him over with the "pick me" mentality, or I would go into my shell and become more depressed and withdrawn. I don't think he cared which one it was really. I began to have a niggle in the back of my mind that he had maybe done the same thing to his ex? He always said she started out looking beautiful having her hair and nails done all the time. Always getting spray tans and new bags and shoes, all paid for by him of course. He tells me this narrative, the one he loves to tell where he's painted as the good guy and she's at fault. She loved his money not him, she used him as a bank machine.

Then she stopped and became withdrawn and started wanting to lie in bed all day with the curtains closed. I was beginning to feel a lot like that myself lately and found the niggle harder and harder to ignore. What if HE made her that way? Wore her down with nasty comments and mind games until she gave up?

I've played right into his hands really, because now I've pretty much said I don't want to know what goes on behind my back. I'm almost condoning it it's like a free pass or a get out of jail card. If some girl pops up at any time in the future he can now say "Oh but you said not to tell you so I didn't tell you!"

One thing about a pathological narcissist is you can never win! No matter how hard you try, how many tactics, how many times you play the game. You are a loser before you even begin.

The only way to win against a narcissist is to never have one in your life.

I had never heard of the word though so I just go deeper and deeper into myself, trying to make sense of it all and trying to tread cautiously around him on egg shells because there's so many different things which trigger him off these days. So many things I could say or do which will cause a fight. I hate fighting and spend all of my energy every day trying to ensure a fight doesn't happen but it always does.

And when it does it's always my fault.

In between the photos of the other girls he likes to send me ones of me when we first met. I look so much happier, healthier, I've got a real glow about me. He likes to send me them to remind me how good things were back at the beginning and if I just do more and try harder I might be able to win him back to the boyfriend he was at the beginning.

He's only the way he is because of the things I say and do that make him this way. If I change then he will treat me better. That's the message behind it all. I'm close to giving up. I can't take much more of this. The name calling has become a regular thing too. Stupid is his favourite one.

"What did you do that for? That was so stupid!"

"Why did you say that? That was a stupid thing to do"

So as well as feeling inadequate in most every other way I'm also dumb as fuck and not capable of rudimentary things. He's far superior to me and should be given more opportunity to micromanage my life for me, make decisions on what I should do, think or say because let's face it I will just fuck it up if I act of my own accord without his guidance.

One day I happen to glance across and there's a blonde girl messaging him.

It's happening in real time in front of me, not like the usual photos etc when I'm back home so I ask who is she? It's just some girl who's asking him for advice about her dog's sore paw, nothing to worry about, so I say OK, fair enough but something about it seems off. I make a mental note to look her up when he's not watching. From what I can gather from her social media she's very flirtatious, outgoing and raunchy. Most of her photos are in revealing clothes and bikinis. I ask him if she's still messaging and he says yes but they're just chatting about dogs. I put my foot down and tell him I don't like it and I'd prefer if he didn't. He plays the I said not to tell me when girls message so he didn't card. I knew he would always play that one so I say yes but now I do know and I don't like her and I want him to cut the chat off if it becomes anything more. I've seen a few of her social media interactions and she seems like trouble with a capital T.

A guy we both know writes a post on an internet dog group about her being a marriage wrecker and a slut. I show him the message and he responds by saying well people could say the same about me couldn't they? That's the way karma works, I've no right to be annoyed after all I had an affair so I should just zip it or he'll start up on that subject and we don't want that do we now? I must be jealous of her because she's younger than me and better looking. It's a punch to the guts and I start to feel threatened so I ask again for him to end the chit chats with her and he reluctantly agrees while making me feel like I've asked him to do something really difficult.

One day she has the cheek to send me a friend request to which I reply "Who is this???" she doesn't reply, which makes me suspicious. Surely a genuine person would introduce themselves? My alarm bells are ringing.

Another day when he's back home he tentatively asks me if I still don't want to know about girls messaging 'cos he thinks I should know about something that's going on. Straight away I know it's her so I say yes, this time I do want to know. He gets annoyed at me for saying yes and then says he will send me what she's sent him but only if I promise not to get angry at him. I promise, through gritted teeth.

He sends me several photos and videos of her masturbating. I'm furious but I've just made a promise not to get angry with him. That promise was always made to be immediately broken. I'm really angry who does she think she is? Why would she just send this out of the blue? There must have been some chat preceding this because you don't just go from having a dog's sore paw chat to full blown porn without there being something else being said or going on in between?

He promises me she just sent them out of the blue and he didn't do anything to solicit them. He says I've broken my promise about getting angry with him so now he can't tell me anymore because he can't bear hearing me so angry and upset. He asks me what I want him to do and

I'm now raging because surely it's obvious what to do? Tell her you have a girlfriend and you're not interested and block her for fuck sake!

He promises me he will but I notice it takes him a few days to get rid of her. He says she was really obsessed with having him and kept sending messages on WhatsApp saying one way or another she was going to have her wicked way with him. It turns out she was the threesome friend of the red head girl, or so he says. I check her entire friend's list and can't find the girl anywhere. I have this horrible gnawing gut feeling, which if I were in a stronger place mentally would make me say, do you know what I don't think this is working, I need some space. It's not you, it's me. (Except it totally is him!)

I ask him to please block her on there too and eventually she will take the hint and find someone else to chase after. He reluctantly agrees to but makes me feel as though I'm asking him to give something up he doesn't want to. He says he's not tempted by her cos she's a slutty type who anybody could easily have. He likes me because I'm hard to get but I really should be more like her in private because

I'm not flinging myself at him the way I should be. Really I should be so glad to have such a loyal boyfriend who manages not to cheat on me whilst getting so many offers from attractive young women.

He tells me he doesn't want the videos and photos on his phone - what do I want him to do with them? I say delete them of course. Then, in a moment of clarity, too many alarm bells going off to ignore, I ask him to screenshot me the conversation so I can see for myself that she genuinely did send him a video out of the blue. Call me old fashioned but it just did not seem plausible to me that a woman would send a video of herself with a monster dildo inside her after a ten minute chat about dogs. I certainly wouldn't but then women are wild these days, up for anything and everything, he loved to tell me.

Too late! He's deleted the conversation like I asked him to. Why would I need to see it don't I trust him? He's been more honest than any other man would be and I have the audacity to not trust him? I say well maybe I should message her and tell her I've seen the videos. He goes mental and says if I do that his life will be over, guys must never break guy code and be honest with their partners, the only exception to this is if they get caught and have to be honest. He's a one in a million honest man and if I message her, he'll be a laughing stock and he'll never be able to tell me anything ever again. I am dumbfounded. He might have me really run down but I am just like "What the fuck??" Sensing he's close to triggering me to end things, he kicks off on one of his rants, turning the whole thing around on me saying I'm one to talk about anyone after what I did in the past, and who I did it with, then he hangs up abruptly, leaving me in tears.

I know what you're thinking, why the hell didn't I just call time on this appalling relationship right there and then. I've asked myself this so many times. I think I was so invested in it I was determined she wasn't going to have him and at the same time so beaten down emotionally that I thought my only two options were to try harder to make it work or just endure things as best I could in the hope they would improve.

She seems to disappear and I breathe a sigh of relief.

Until the morning of my surgery that is.

I'm driving myself to the hospital and he's sitting beside me so he can drive my car home and look after the dogs until I'm well enough to be released. Normally the hospital stay for major surgery like this is a few days and it's a 12 week recovery period so he's agreed to stay and look after the dogs and me until I'm well enough and physically recovered enough to cope with everything on my own.

He's on his phone, as always. Glued to it like a life support machine. I often feel like there's something not right going on but any time I say "What you up to?" He'll say "Just chatting to Terry" or some other male friend and that's the end of the conversation.

On this particular morning I glance across and it says he's chatting to a male name he told me was a workmate but it's not him. It's a video of a naked girl and I recognise her immediately.

I slam on the brakes and pull over. This needs to be dealt with right now, this shit needs sorting.

I've literally got about 15 minutes to figure out what's going on, any longer and I'll be late for my surgery. I've not slept properly in days and am sick with worry as it is. I have terrible white coat syndrome and having never had surgery before I'm absolutely bricking it.

I demand to know what's going on!

He tells me she just sent him it out of the blue, I demand to see it and it's a video of her naked brushing her teeth over a sink in the gym. That alone is weird enough that anyone would make a video of themselves doing that but I'm most interested in the conversation surrounding it. His reply to her video is "LOL". I demand to know how she's even on there because he promised me he blocked her. He doesn't answer, he doesn't have one because he knows he's caught out. One lie leads to another lie and so on. He tries to justify it saying he hasn't said or done anything to encourage her look! He wrote "LOL" with no kisses or anything like he writes on my messages but I'm absolutely fuming. I'm having none of his bullshit this time. I call him straight out on it and ask if they are having sex, he says no of course not she's a cokehead slut no way he would put his dick in that, everyone's been there. He likes to laugh at how desperate she is. I say what, at my expense?? Surely if she knows your taken and you continue to let her send this stuff she must think she's in with a chance? You might not be encouraging her but you're not exactly discouraging her either. He points out were now running late, that I shouldn't get so stressed before my surgery and we should discuss it afterwards.

This is so far from ideal it's unreal but I know I have to get moving so we spend the rest of the half hour drive to the infirmary arguing like cat and dog over what's just occurred. He's being somewhat apologetic saying he's in the wrong he shouldn't have unblocked her but then turning it around in the same breath. It's all my fault because I made him feel emasculated by asking him to block her instead of just letting him handle it in his own way like a normal man would. I really need to stop making so many demands on him, I'm lucky to have him when there's all these women just dying to take my place!

I'm so angry I can't even look at him as we arrive and he leaves me in the waiting room. I feel so betrayed, my alarm bells are ringing ten to the dozen and after months of worrying about the 1 in 1000 chance of dying during the operation, I'm now feeling like my life is so rubbish maybe that would be for the best.

My sister has driven up from England to be with me during and after the op and as soon as he leaves I collapse into her arms in floods of tears. She doesn't know what's wrong and thinks it's just pre-op nerves. He's met my friends and family and they all think he's wonderful 'cos he showed them the side he showed me for the first 6 months. We look so good together when were out in public, the charade has been kept up so well, if anyone did ask me if things were ok, I'm not sure I could bring myself to tell them, I feel so humiliated right now.

I don't have time to tell her what's really been going on, it's time for me to get into my gown and meet my surgeon, or should I say surgeons because they have brought specialists in for this operation as it's not your usual everyday routine hysterectomy. No, I had to go one better than that and make things far more complicated than they needed to be.

Chapter 17

Heaven or Hell?

I wake from my surgery and straight away two things hit me head on. One is the excruciating deferred pain in my shoulder, which I was warned about prior to my op but you don't realise just how sore it's going to be. The second was that I was alive. I had survived a risky operation and now had to face all the horrible stuff I'd been experiencing these past few years, and most importantly, deal with the ramifications of what had happened just prior to my operation.

Waves of emotion come over me and I start crying. I'm crying not tears of joy for surviving, but tears of grief because I didn't want to wake up. Waking up means I have to go to Plan B. The kind nurses tell me it's perfectly normal to feel this way after this type of surgery and I'm sure they just chalk it down to my hormones playing havoc. I'm wheeled off into a private room where I'll spend the next few days recuperating until I'm strong enough to go home.

The trouble is my mind is racing ten to the dozen going over every single thing that's happened in my so-called relationship and I spend the time I'm supposed to be resting questioning everything, asking myself "How did I get here? How on earth did I allow myself to let things get this bad?"

I had endured years of subtle, and not so subtle emotional manipulation and abuse, gaslighting and mind game playing to the extent that neither of my voices were there to guide me in any decision making processes anymore. I had basically relived the role I watched my Mother live as a child, the same one that angered and disgusted me. I had become her. He had become my Dad. Ugh, the thought of that made me sick! I had tread so very, very carefully around him to try to avoid any triggers that might set off arguments. I had made myself so small, insignificant and non-threatening to try to minimise his outbursts and just get through each day without a barney of some kind. Nothing I did made any difference. He was on a one way course hellbent to control me, abuse me, destroy me.

Somewhere along the line Angel started to whisper to me that it wasn't right the way I was being treated, I needed to get out. Devil had a solution to the problem. Just kill yourself. I'm sick of living on your shoulder, you'd be doing us both a favour! Take lots of pills and go to sleep and never wake up. You're a big, useless coward anyway so you won't have the guts to hang yourself or cut yourself, nothing dramatic like that for you, so just overdose and end it all, you just want it all to stop don't you?

I find myself listening to both voices and the one thing that stops me every single time from following Devil's plan is my dogs. I love them to bits, they're the only thing that keeps me going every day, I can't leave them behind surely? Who would look after them? Plus Angel quietly reminds me that people who commit suicide are irredeemable in God's eyes, remember what I was taught when I was younger? Judas Iscariot betrayed Jesus and then couldn't cope with the guilt so he hung himself. He's not getting any second chances. He won't be there in the paradise with a pet panda or a fruit laden banquet table. Don't be a Judas!

There is a way you can get out of this though.

Don't forget that if you refuse blood in your surgery and you die, then you die a martyr for God and he'll instantly forgive you for all your sins. JW's call it "taking the underground" it means you die but it's really just like closing your eyes for a second and dozing off then you wake up in the paradise. Womb fully restored, no more back pain, no more any pain of any kind. Everyone around you will be lovely, no more name calling or mind games. Friendly animals, beautiful scenery, a nice log cabin in the woods.

I remember all the times as a kid when Mum wouldn't let me have certain medical treatments or vaccinations. She would scan the ingredients on food packaging to make sure there wasn't any trace of anything that might contain blood, even going as far as to avoid the colourant cochineal as it contained crushed beetle shells. If the beetle hadn't had its throat slit and the blood properly drained then you were in God's bad books!

Scriptures about refusing to eat or drink blood came back to mind and I remembered Mum's words that it was better to die and have God's favour than to take blood and lose it. I had a lot of sins to be forgiven for already, my Judgement scroll was very long, it was going to take Jesus a long time to read everything I'd done wrong in my life as he sat down on his huge celestial throne. If I die a martyr during my surgery it's a win - win situation, I go straight to paradise and I don't have to put up with all the horrible stuff I'm currently putting up with. I don't know what fucked up so badly in the hard wiring of my brain to make me think this was a good plan but I decided this was my path. Just making this decision for myself felt good. It was liberating not to have to run this past Mr Nasty who wanted to know my every move and have his input on it. No this was something I was keeping to myself. Devil pipes up that I should really have a plan B. Stock up on plenty of pills just in case I make it through the surgery. Angel pipes back that Plan B is for me to pluck up the courage and leave him, despite all his petty threats.

Not only has he been brow beating me for so long about my affair with Mr Man to the point where the mere mention of anything connected to him begins to give me the judders, but lately he's taken to using it as a threat.

"Why don't you tell his wife?"

"You must be scared of him to never have told her about you, why don't you tell her?"

I firmly argue that its old water under an even older bridge and going and telling his wife we had an affair will only cause unnecessary drama. If, on the other hand, she found out somehow by other means and contacted me, then yes, I would be honest and tell her, but why the need to go poking the hornet's nest?

"But wouldn't YOU want to know if it were you? Doesn't she deserve to know? You must still hold a torch for him if you won't tell her?"

He would go on and on about it, until it became this thing he would use to pick a fight on a regular basis. I must still be madly in love with him or else I would have gone and told his wife by now? Maybe he will go and tell his wife for me.

It might sound trivial on this page but every time he did this I would get so stressed out and feel so desperately trapped. Like an animal caught up in a cage I would frantically search for ways to pacify him, change the subject, anything at all to escape the shame, fear, disgust and degradation that I was feeling. We went through a lot of fights and a lot of mind games to get to the point where he had broken me down enough to be able to treat me this way, but we finally reached rock bottom where I would just sit there and endure his rants about how disgusting I was, how could I? imagine having sex with that old man, it repulsed him to have sex with me now and I was never going to find any man who would ever take me seriously, love me the way he had, want to marry me or view me as special. I was forever soiled by my past and this relationship was the best I could possibly hope for. If I did dare to consider leaving he would expose me and cause lots of drama for me. After all my ex had been in the press recently for several violent offences and was serving prison time for hitting a woman. He hadn't treated me this way when I was with him, but if he or I told his wife we had an affair I would be the first person he would come looking for when he got out.

I began having panic attacks again on a regular basis, some days it was hard to breathe or think straight. I had managed to overcome them when I was younger with the help of therapy, now they were back with a vengeance. One day I plucked up the courage to go to the Doctor's and I collapsed in a heap on the driveway. A kind nurse came out and gathered me up and asked me if I was OK. I blurted out no I wasn't I wanted to die. There I had actually said it out loud to someone, it was real now and not just inside my head.

I didn't want to die of course. I just didn't want to carry on living the nightmare I felt trapped within. I think a lot of people who experience suicidal ideation don't actually want to die, they just don't want to live the way they are currently living and frantically look for a quick fix solution. I didn't feel like I had much to live for other than my daily routine looking after the dogs, but death is so final and there was all the religious indoctrination swirling around in the big ugly mess inside my brain.

The nurse was lovely and referred me to see a doctor who would then put me on a ten step therapy program to help me work through how I was feeling. It was hard to get this set up as it was a male therapist and while we managed to arrange the first couple of sessions, it then became hard to continue them as Mr Nasty was around and he couldn't hear me talking to some guy on the phone, there was no way I could talk about the things he was saying or doing to me in front of a strange man either. I'd be accused of having an affair with yet another man I hadn't, it just wasn't worth the risk. So I missed a few sessions and then had to be re-referred and start the process over again but eventually I made it through the program. My therapy was all there in black and white on my worksheets. My therapist concluded there was nothing "wrong" with me per say, I was in an abusive relationship and needed to get out, as quickly as possible before he could damage me more.

He referred me to several women's help groups and that was all he could do for me so now it was up to me. The trouble is, when you're so low, so lacking in self-esteem and confidence and so manipulated by someone, even seeing things in black and white in your own handwriting, sometimes isn't enough to make you take that leap into action.

I lie in my hospital bed thinking of all the red flags, the subtle ones I ignored, the glaring ones I didn't want to see, the ones I dismissed because he had a convenient excuse for each and every one.

I google "Signs of a cheating man" the first article looks interesting. I speed read it, needing to do as much research as possible before I must go home to face the music. It doesn't feel like my home while he's there dominating it, I feel like I want to get my dogs and run, except I've nowhere to run to. I read all 12 of the signs and cry again as I realise he's done or doing all 12 of them. I feel like such a gullible idiot! All those times he would say his phone charger cable was too short or didn't fit my charger so he would go out to his van and chat to people on the phone. His phone that was perpetually on silent with notifications hidden from his home screen and turned face down any time he felt brave enough to leave it alone for a moment. If he popped outside to use it, he would say it was his mate Terry or his daughter. If I popped out to tell him dinner was ready he would scowl at me and hold the phone away secretively or he'd see me coming in the mirror and go "OK Terry good chatting mate got to go now" so I wouldn't be able to ask who he was chatting to. He would take his phone to the toilet and spend ages in there and I couldn't ask what he was doing because that's just wrong to ask someone why they're taking so long to poo isn't it? I'm such an unreasonable person, so paranoid, why do I have such an issue with all the women who comment things on his Facebook like "Happy Birthday Gorgeous" or "Hey sexy" it's just a laugh and I should "Wise up" "Chill out" "Stop being such a drama queen"

I just feel like such a fool!

He's coming to visit me this afternoon and I am brimming over with emotions, mostly dread but lots of anger too. I have questions, so many questions!

My blood pressure is all over the place, the nurses keep coming in and out taking it all the time. I'm bleeding too much from my wound and they can't work out why. I should have stopped bleeding by now. They call the surgeon back to inspect my wound and she says I haven't been properly cauterised so I must have another surgery to fix it. I'm soon crying again because even though I beg them to take me back down to theatre and put me under again, they're not able to do that. The special surgeons who were called in for my bloodless surgery have left. She reminds me once again that I had a very risky procedure having bloodless surgery and that I was warned by her several times prior to the op that my risk of dying would be increased. Each time she said it, it only served to make me more determined that this was the right path to choose. I had one person in my life trying to fearmonger my every decision and that was plenty. I didn't need another one.

I've to have the second surgery awake, under a local anaesthetic. This feels as terrifying if not more than when they wheeled me into the theatre for the general one. I was paralysed by fear the minute I rolled through those double doors and saw the huge team standing around me. I felt so small and alone. The kind nurse rubbed my shoulder sensing how tense I was and tried to get me to lie back and relax. The last thing I remember was Mr Nasty's last words to me before he left. I'd begged him to please not let one of my dogs off the lead as I was worried she might run off. If she did he might get stressed and just drive off and leave her. Or worse if she came back he might beat her harshly as I'd watched him do to his own dogs when they misbehaved. He had said I should stop being such a drama queen and a worrier and that she would be fine to be let off the lead. I worry too much about stupid dogs.

I try to sit up and shout out that they must please make sure he doesn't let her off the lead! And then I slide into the deep, black depths of unconsciousness.

No such oblivion for me this time around. I must now face Mr Nasty and then have the next surgery, I'm not sure which to dread most.

He duly arrives as my sister is leaving. She's been a rock to me, so supportive and although I've only shared some brief details of what's really been going on, she promises me that I have done a really good, honourable and brave thing and I'll be rewarded for it. I've "Made a firm stand for Jehovah" she tells me and that means everything will get easier from now on now I've picked my side in the battle of Good versus Evil.

She means well of course, but things are about to get a whole heap worse before they get better!

I can't control my anger for long and within minutes of Mr Nasty sitting down in the chair next to my bed with that smug look on his face I've grown to loathe, we are fighting like cat and dog again. I am fuming he has betrayed me by unblocking her and why is she sending him videos of herself in the buff? Surely when he blocked her that time ages ago when she sent the dildo video she would have taken the hint and not sent anymore?

He confesses he has had her unblocked for ages because he gets a sick thrill over her going to more and more desperate measures to try to entice him into bed. I tell him he is sick and I don't want to be with someone who treats women like that. When I get home as soon as I'm well enough to look after the dogs I want him packed up and gone. I feel a surge of bravery but its short lived. He starts apologising and says "Look I've blocked her now surely that's enough?" he shows me her blocked on his phone and deletes the conversation, he shows me her blocked everywhere else so she can't Facebook, ring or text him too. No, it's not enough! I don't trust him now. Trust is precious it's like glass once its broken you can glue it back together all you like but it'll never be the same again. His apologies quickly turn to anger and he finds a way to turn it all around on me.

How dare I accuse him of doing something he hasn't done when I had an affair? I've had this thrown at me so many times I'm sick to the back teeth of it now.

I bawl back at him that I'm sick of this and his threats, yes I had an affair, it was over long before I met him, I've never done anything like that ever again and no plans to. I've never so much as looked at another man the whole time we've been together, never mind have cosy chats with one or receive wanking videos! He needs to stop with this and he needs to stop right now I'm done with this shit.

Seeing that I mean business this time he leaves telling me if I carry on like this he will just leave right now and not look after the dogs as agreed, plus he will go to Mr Man's house and tell his wife about our affair.

He has me over a barrel once again. The dogs mean the world to me, I tell him he can do what he likes but for their sake just go home and look after them until I'm well enough to come home then we'll sort what happens after that. He stomps off in a huff. It's at this moment I realise this man really does not give one single shit about anyone except himself.

He leaves and I start panicking, what if he does just leave and the poor dogs are going mad, no food, no water, nobody to let them out? I'm crying again, my blood pressures sky high and the nurses are back, almost the minute he leaves. I guess they must have heard us arguing. They ask if I'm OK and I tell them no, I'm trapped in a relationship with an absolute bastard of a man, that man that just left and I can't cope with all of this right now. They give me pain relief and tell me someone will come and chat to me soon. It's all going to be OK. I wish I could feel reassured but I don't.

I press my morphine driver over and over until it runs out. The nurses come and tell me off for pressing it so much. I roll in and out of being in agony screaming out for pain relief and sleeping an unrefreshing sleep. Every time I press the button I imagine it as a button which will inject me with something to end all of this. I have no motivation to do anything, the nurses come and force me to get up out of bed, go to the toilet, take a short walk around the room before I go back to bed. I must try to poop and fart to get rid of all the gas. I'll feel better once I do and I can't go home until I can poop. A nice nurse comes and persuades me to get up and have a shower and I cry in the shower because she's kind to me. I wish I could be kind to myself. All I want is to get back into bed and keep pressing that button until it all goes away. When they come to take it away I cry some more and try to hang onto it.

A tiny, young woman wearing a hijab comes and sits beside my bed to talk to me. She's worried I'm in a domestic abuse situation and tells me there's help there if I need it. She presses a card into my hand and tells me to hide it in my bag and look at it later if that works best. She's got kind eyes and I start crying again. I think to myself she looks so young, what can she possibly know about domestic abuse? But I remind myself that if some of my friends knew what I had been putting up with they would be truly shocked. I'm supposed to be this strong, independent, take no shit from anybody type of woman and here I am lying in a hospital bed wishing my life away. I do take her advice though, the card must be hidden, it will only give Mr Nasty an excuse to start another fight.

I get a message from him and he tells me he's at Mr Man's house. Apparently he's not in prison anymore. I'm not allowed to look him up on

Google because if I do that means I'm still in love with him so I have to rely on what Mr Nasty tells me Mr Man is up to these days. I don't actually care or want to know what he's up to but oh, I get the updates regardless of whether I want them or not! I sometimes used to bite back and say that Mr Nasty is the only person in this relationship who's obsessed with Mr Man 'cos I certainly am not, but this just causes more fights so eventually I stop saying it. I'm still thinking it though.

He tells me he's outside his door and he's going to fight him in the street if he comes out. My first thought is that I've had about enough of this as I can handle and I hope Mr Man just comes out and beats the hell out of him. But who is going to look after the dogs if he does? So I begin to panic, help me out Angel and Devil what do I do now? Come on, I never ask for your advice, not once ever in all these years but I'm asking you both now, what do I do?

Devil is quick to respond. Tell him to "Fuck off" and block him.

Good advice actually considering this is Devil were talking about.

Angel isn't far behind with "I think he's lying, shall we set a trap to see if he is? I think it would be good for you to catch him in a lie so it takes away his power over you"

"Yes! great idea OK so how do I do this"? Angel quickly guides me through what to do. I should message my nice neighbour and ask her could she please take a quick look and see if his van and my car are both at the house? She's going to want to know what's going on so just tell her somethings going on and you'll explain later but if she can tell you one way or the other it's going to really help you.

She quickly obliges and both vehicles are there. So that means only one thing as Mr Man lives a half hour's drive away. It means the lying bastard is lying on the couch sending me messages deliberately to hurt, upset, anger and fearmonger me, knowing full well I'm lying here in a hospital bed trying to avoid stress, and trying to rest to lower my sky high blood pressure.

This revelation is the first step in me taking back the control he has over me. Suddenly I began to see the sick individual I'm actually dealing with. The threats began to lose their hold. I feel somewhat calmer. I message back saying I'm really upset he's done this, but is he OK?

After a long pause, no doubt to think of which lies to tell next to give the best impact, he replied that his wife came to the door and said he wasn't in, but that he was going to go back another day and ask him for a "square go" which is Scottish slang for a punch up in the street, gypsy bare knuckle style.

I wrote back "please don't! Please just go home and look after the dogs until I get out and we will try to sort this". It kills me to beg and plead. I've done that so many times but now seeing through the deceptive fog, I can play a pleading groveller if it gets me what I want.

He agrees to. I feel like I have the upper hand knowing that I know he's lying, but he doesn't know that I know. I'm not sure yet what my next move is going to be, but what I do know is I need to survive, stay alive, win this fight. No more Mrs sit down and take it. No more woe is me, my life isn't worth living. It is, even if only to get home and see my dogs and give them big hugs. This bastard is NOT getting the better of me.

I thank my neighbour and promise to tell her what's going on when I get home. She's intrigued, just as I would be if the situation were reversed, she won't be happy with a brush off and I've pulled her into this so she deserves some sort of explanation. Plus it would be nice to have a bit of female support on hand for what is going to be a really testing time when I do go home.

I finally fall into a reasonably restful sleep and wake the next morning feeling scared but determined to extract myself from this deadbeat man and our toxic relationship.

Chapter 18

Healing

I can poop and shower unaided, and they need the bed for someone else, so it's time for me to leave.

I've been dreading this but there's just no getting around it. When I arrive home it's so painful just doing simple things like getting out of the car door, climbing the stairs, getting comfortable in bed. I underestimated just how much post op pain I was going to be in. I have meds to take every 4 hours and 2 hours plus a heat pad I'm not supposed to use too much but I have it pressed onto my wound as much as I can bear, to try to distract myself from the throbbing agony. I am determined to get out of this awful fix I've gotten myself into but I'm nowhere near able to do anything at all where the dogs are concerned, so I need him and he knows it. He's being all nice and apologetic and sickly sweet, trying to build things back up again while I'm just trying to get through each hour of the day wincing in pain and either sleeping or pretending to sleep when he's around. When I'm pretending to sleep he leaves me alone and it buys me time to think up my great escape plan. I try to picture what I will do and say and how I will stick to it. A lot of the time though the thought of it all scares me so I hoard most of it onto the "Deal with Later when I'm feeling stronger" shelf.

Friends and family come to visit which is an immense source of comfort. He doesn't stick around much while they're there which normally he would so I think everyone senses things are not good. My neighbour comes to visit and I tell her the brief jist of what's gone down. She tells me she's there for me anytime I need to chat and that I can get through this, everyone's behind me, if I need any help at all just ask. I need to get rid of him though, he shouldn't be treating me like this.

My best friend comes to visit and this is the visit I've been looking forward to and dreading the most in equal measures. She's a no nonsense straight talker that's why we get along so well, she is not going to pull any punches whatsoever when I tell her what's been happening. He slinks out the door the minute she arrives and makes sure he stays gone the whole time she's here.

I break down and tell her what's been going on. She tells me she's noticed me becoming introverted and not having my usual cheery disposition. She knew something was wrong but not exactly what. She tells me in no uncertain terms I need to get rid of him and I need to do it right now! Where are his bags? She will pack them and put them on the doorstep and she'll sit with me when he comes back. If he starts anything she will call the cops. She also offers to take over looking after the dogs as she can see how tied I am to him while he's here doing it.

She's right in everything she says and I so want to be strong enough to take her advice, Devil and Angel are both in agreement they both want him gone. Ultimately for slightly different reasons but at the end of the day they both want me to be happy and he's making me miserable. Angel wants me to have deep, meaningful, spiritual happiness and Devil wants me to have wild parties and decadent sex starting the minute my stitches have healed. None of these are going to happen with him in the picture so he needs to get gone.

I try so hard to summon up the courage to go along with her plan, it does make so much sense, but I just cant. I feel so weak both physically and mentally so I promise her I will leave him I'm just not strong enough to do it yet. She's got my back though and she's just a quick phone call away if I need her. Everyone needs a friend like this. Thank God for her sensible advice. I know I didn't take it immediately, I hesitated and stalled and panicked many times before seeing it through, but knowing she and others were there for me really helped me.

As the days turn into weeks I start to get stronger and my pain lessens, enabling me to sleep through the night instead of waking up groaning in agony at 4am. I need to start making this exit strategy happen because the longer you leave something the harder it is to do it.

One day he has a particularly difficult phone call with his daughter and for the first time ever takes part of the call with me present in the room which I'm shocked at. At a later date the real reason becomes apparent but I overhear a very distressed sounding young girl crying down the phone saying "Daddy, please come home"! I don't know her, I've only ever seen photos of her she looks a very stunningly beautiful young woman who has a great career ahead of her so it's distressing to hear her upset like this. He doesn't give me many details after the call ends just that there's some issue with her boyfriend and he needs to go home for work anyway as his leave is coming to an end so can I manage Ok on my own from here?

I most definitely can and start to feel excited at the prospect of finally getting to sort this giant mess out once and for all, from the comfort of my home without him breathing down my neck as he'll be hundreds of miles away.

My phone pings and it's his ex-partner. She's looked me up on Facebook and wants to speak to me. I show him and say before I talk to her, is there anything you want to tell me? He begs me not to open the message and speak to her, it will only cause lots of grief. She's a psycho (so he says) and she's been bombarding him with messages about his daughter for days. He eventually blocked her and that culminated in the daughter's phone call.

This is his version of events, which couldn't be further from the truth but at this present moment do I want to add another sprinkling of stress to spice up my chaos cocktail? As usual, advice is just a voice in my head away.

Angel says wait 'til he leaves then talk to her, you have nothing to lose!

Devil says fuck the pair of them, he's bad enough with his own drama do you really need hers too? Just get rid of him and the rest will solve itself.

Devil seems to offer the solution which will help my stress levels the most right now so I go with that plan and leave the message sitting in my requests box. Big Mistake! But then I've made so many they are beginning to blur into each other, it's hard to see the wood for the trees.

He goes home, apparently to his mother's to wash his clothes for work, to see his daughter and then to do a painting job for an old farmer who lives beside his sister's holiday home in the south of Ireland. He's been here before last summer to do a painting job for his sister and we weren't able to chat much then as the signal was so bad, so I know in advance what he's about to say but he says it anyway.

"Don't forget there's no signal down there, but don't worry I'll make sure I talk to you every day to check your OK even if I need to climb up the top of the cliffs to get one bar"

In a normal, healthy relationship this would feel sweet, comforting and a sign that someone cares, but everything he says and does now just feels so fake, his voice gives me the "ick" and I don't believe a word that comes out of his mouth, but I play along for now as my master exit plan is just around the corner.

It's crazy now to look back on all of this and ask myself why did I feel the need to get further "proof" that he was a wrong 'un? Why didn't I just block him, change the locks, cut contact and get rid the minute he left my house to drive home. I don't know how or why I justified it to myself, as if everything he had put me through up until this moment wasn't enough reason to sack him for good, I felt like I needed some concrete evidence that he couldn't worm or lie his way around that I could use to dump him for good and never look back.

I didn't have to wait very long.

One day I spot him chatting to a girl from England on social media and arranging to meet up with her next time he's over. I see red and I am determined this is the straw that broke the camel's back. He either thinks I'm stupid and he can get away with any behaviour now because I haven't kicked him to the curb, or he genuinely thinks I haven't seen this so it's OK, what I don't know can't hurt me.

I feel so ridiculous writing this now as it sounds ludicrous but this whole time I had his Facebook password. At any point in time I could have easily gone and snooped to see what he was up to, probably saving myself a lot of pain as I would have found out far faster who he really was, but in my defence I'm not that type of person I would hate it if someone felt that amount of mistrust in me. I don't think I would want to be in a relationship with someone who felt the need to snoop through my private stuff. I always took what he said to me on trust. Stupid and naïve of me, but that's why I never looked, even though oftentimes both Angel and Devil would goad me to have a quick peek.

This time there was no going back. I logged in and clicked on his messages expecting to see filthy ones exchanged between them but surprisingly there were none. What I did find however was one from a girl with the same first name as his daughter but a different surname. Assuming it must be her, I clicked on it, to find it wasn't but that he had sent her messages from a holiday in Iceland he was on with her Mother and that she had lost her phone during the trip. Reeling, I read the messages over and over with shock and anger. It was away back the time he told me he had been painting his sister's house. He had been messaging me saying how much he loved and missed me and couldn't wait to get this job done so he could get home and visit me. All the time he was actually in Iceland with this other woman! Did his sister even have a holiday home? What other lies had he told me? Was everything he had ever told me a lie?

Unless you've been in this predicament it's hard to understand just how foolish and angry you feel. In the case of women who are deeply in love the betrayal discovery is far harder because there is a real hurt to deal with. Fortunately as I was already out of love for Mr Nasty I only had foolishness, humiliation and anger to deal with but they were a potent cocktail of hurt. I message the girl and ask her straight out what's going on with her Mother and my so-called partner of the last 6 ½ years? She messages me back wanting some proof so I send her photos of us together. She tells me that she's sorry but I'm in for a hurtful surprise because he's not only been seeing her Mum for around the same length of time, but he also lives with a woman and has a daughter with another. There's others on the go too. This is just the tip of the iceberg, tarty naked gym girl hasn't even had a mention yet.

Fairplay to the girl, she's very candid, she asks me when was the last time we spoke and I tell her just a few hours ago! I show her the message he sent about the painting job and having to climb up the cliffs so he could text me. She tells me straight the only cliffs he's anywhere near are the Grand Canyon as he and her Mother are on holiday right now in the States.

I'm absolutely seething and reeling. I find her Mother on Facebook and message her to ask what's going on? I also look through his block list and see a list of female names, two in particular stand out. One is his ex the other is a name I don't recognise but the minute I look at her photo I see it's his daughter. This is odd? Why does she have a completely different name? I message the other woman's daughter back with a photo he sent me of him and his daughter together and ask why she has a different name to the one he told me? She replies saying that girl is not his real daughter, she's his step daughter, he lives with her Mother. They've been together for about 23 years, he treats her like shit and his real daughter lives somewhere else with her Mother.

Confused? That's how I felt too. What a mess, a huge web of lies. I don't really know how to process this but I know this is all the "proof" I need so I message him telling him I know about his affair, I call him out on all of it and tell him we're done, I block him don't ever want to see or hear from him ever again!

The punches keep coming as the day goes on, emotional blow after blow. The girl from the photo gets in touch she's actually lovely, she's his step daughter, we chat on the phone for 3 hours, she can't understand why he gave his real daughter's name to her other than he must have been trying to make sure I was never able to look any of them up on social media or contact them to ask questions. Pretty much everything he ever told me was a lie. It was both therapeutic and shameful to listen to. I felt like such a bloody idiot! I wanted to literally whack myself over the head with something for being such a numpty and swallowing all of this crap for so long, whilst at the same time letting him grind me down to the point I felt life wasn't worth living. All the while he was living it up with some other woman on expensive holidays all around the world.

She tells me I've not to beat myself up he did the same thing to her Mother, for far longer and it took her Mother years to break free from the grip he had over her, but she did and now she's all the better for it. She tells me about the day she rang him and I heard her crying. Her Mother had found out he was having an affair with both me, and the woman he was currently on holiday with. If only I had read her message that day, I could have found out the way I was meant to! She promises me one day I will be the same, I will look back on all of this like a bad dream and be a stronger, wiser woman for it. I seem like a nice genuine person and she wishes me well. As parting advice she asks me if I have seen a new series that's just appeared on Netflix. I haven't yet but it's on my to watch list. She tells me to go home and watch it. It will help. It's a true story about a con man who lies and cheats various women and eventually gets stabbed to death by one of their daughters. They even share the same name. She tells me the similarities are chilling so I head home and binge watch it all in one night. She tells me the name of the series is his nickname back in Ireland. He's a thrill seeker, pathological liar and a serial cheat. I still watch it from time to time to remind myself just how easy it is for men to lie and creep their way into women's lives and then devastate them.

I decide there and then I'm never getting back with him ever no matter what he says or does. I'm never going near another man ever again and I'm going to get through this and come out the other side victorious. I simply have to there's nothing else for it.

The holiday woman gets in touch, she is cheeky and doesn't seem to care, she says she knows he lives with someone else so what? She seems to think I'm some kind of psycho and she had him first so I tell her she's as fucked up as him, she's welcome to him and I block her too. Drama,

drama, drama that's all this man has ever brought into my life. It's time I took some control back.

Their holiday ends and the contact starts, he's blocked so all he can do is leave me answer machine messages. He leaves 57 in total. All different variations of him begging me to take him back, to give him a second chance, please don't dump him just because of one silly mistake. It was just a drunken one night stand, she meant nothing to him, she dragged him into bed and raped him, she begged him to go on holiday with her multiple times and bought his ticket for him, how could any man refuse all of that? blah blah blah blah blah.

Eventually, realising all his schemes to get me back are failing he threatens something he knows will really tug at my heart strings. I have a friend who committed suicide and he knows this so he plays this trump card. I wonder if it's just a ploy? Devil tells me he's just saying it to play me and to ignore him, Angel says what if he's not do you want that on your conscience if he does do something stupid?

Because of this threat I stay in communication with him for far longer than I should have. I'm ashamed to write these paragraphs, this whole chapter to be honest. I really should have just cut contact but he seemed so genuine, all the tears the begging and sobbing wore me down. I think he knew exactly what he was doing and he just picked away at all my defences until he found the one that would allow him a sneaky way back into my life.

During this time, the other woman gets back in touch. Her attitude has changed dramatically since the last time we spoke. He's been making her life hell with threats, taunts, name calling, head games, you name it. I reluctantly agree to talk to her and the revelations which come out are just like blow after blow of humiliation. It's therapeutic for both of us to compare notes though. To know that he told both of us lies about where he was, who he was with, what he was doing. We compare our timelines and share experiences. Two strangers who would never otherwise be connected only for this vile, lying narcissist who suckered both of us into his evil web. I start to feel compassion towards her. I have a head start on her as far as the healing process goes. They have been together much longer, she's known him her whole life, she also stayed with him after I got in touch to reveal he had been cheating on us both. She bought into his lies that I was some crazed, psychopathic woman, obsessed with him and on a revenge mission, except she didn't really deep down because as the saying goes a woman is always the first to know, but the last to find out. Her intuition coupled with the numerous photos I sent her daughter as "proof" showed we had been in a romantic relationship for far longer than he was trying to make out. He was even wearing a shirt she had bought him in one photo with me, and the same in one of her photos of him with her, he was wearing one of my tops. The sheer audacity of the man was just unfathomable.

I began my recovery process, gradually withdrawing further and further back from having contact with him, telling myself if he does kill himself it is **NOT** my fault. He tries to blame me for his real daughter finding out that he used the photos of his far prettier stepdaughter to hide the fact he was in another relationship when we met. His poor daughter understandably feels really hurt and betrayed. She contacts me and we chat, she seems like a lovely young woman, this man honestly does not deserve all these great people in his circle. I start to think he actually deserves to be on his own, miserable, lonely and bitter for the rest of his days, although I wouldn't wish suicide on anyone having seen the devastation it causes. Devil says the world would be a better place without people like him in it. Devil is ruthless and pulls no punches.

Eventually things come to a head and he starts sending me more and more crazed messages and gets incensed when I don't reply within the time frame he wants me to, or if I change my profile picture, or anything which makes him think I might be moving on. I have a life to live and his suicide threat while it did have some sway when it was fresh, has now worn stale. I have new chapters to write in my life story and he is not welcome in any of them. He was a lesson I learned the hard way and it's made me so much wiser.

I block him again and he sends me the most vile abusive messages I've ever had from anyone my entire life. 16 of them, 14 of which contain threats including death threats and general threats against me, my property and my pets. All 16 of them are really abusive, he's burning the bridge this time and going all out to make sure I know how hated I am for discovering his lies, calling time on it all, revealing all the truths he wanted kept hidden and then having the cheek to put the whole sorry debacle behind me and move on. How very dare I?!?

There are so many more things I could write about what happened to me, chapters I could fill and perhaps I will write some of the stories some other time but for now I'm just glad to be out with some of my sanity still intact. Now it's time to focus on me, learn to forgive myself for making such a whopping mistake and claw back some of the self-esteem I lost by allowing him to treat me so badly for so long. I decide firmly with Angel very much in agreement, that I need a good, wholesome direction for my life to take next, going forwards. Forget all about men and relationships, far too much hassle. I must find a path that will lead me to true happiness. Angel is quick to remind me that there's always God to help out where men fall short. I've tried to find happiness with an assortment of men now, isn't it time I gave up on all that silliness and looked for spiritual happiness instead?

Chapter 19

Hovis Biscuits

On February 16th 1852 in Pennsylvania Charles Taze Russell was born.

Also known as "Pastor Russell" and "Brother Russell" throughout his life, he spent many years searching for what he deemed to be the correct interpretation of the scriptures regarding Christ's invisible return. This led him to begin writing a journal named Zion's Watchtower and Herald of Christ's presence, the first issue of which was published in 1879.

There were many controversies regarding Pastor Russell's writings, teachings, failed end time predictions, business partnerships, business ventures and marital affairs but generally he is regarded by Jehovah's Witnesses today as being the original founding Father of the religion.

In 1881 he founded Zion's Watchtower Tract Society which a few years later became incorporated with Russell as President, the name was then shortened to Watch Tower Bible and Tract society in 1886.

Printing, producing and selling Bibles and Bible related literature was big business back then and the headquarters of the society moved to Brooklyn in 1908 where it remained the headquarters of the Jehovah's Witness religion until 2016 when it was relocated to Warwick, New York.

Throughout Russell's life he made several predictions about Christ's invisible return and his rapture to heaven which he had the fortune, or some might say misfortune, to live long enough to see debunked.

After his death, Joseph Franklin Rutherford took over presidency of the society, amidst many disputes over the election process, in 1917 and adopted the name "Jehovah's Witnesses" in 1931.

This is not intended to be a full and detailed account of Watchtower's entire history, simply a summarised one, there is much information available online about various controversies and scandals involving Rutherford and subsequent Presidents, for there were several successors after him. However, I do think it's important to set the scene for anyone unfamiliar with Witness history. In 1976 the Watchtower Society dispensed with the idea of having a President and Jehovah's Witnesses worldwide came under the direct control of "The Governing Body" which is noteworthy as being a man made business term, found nowhere whatsoever in the Bible.

It's also noteworthy that the Society does not file any publicly accessible financial figures, relies mostly on voluntary donations made by its worldwide membership for funding and uses mainly free voluntary labour for a huge portion of its building and real estate projects.

The term "Bethel" means House of God and Jehovah's Witnesses place the headquarters on a special kind of spiritual pedestal meaning if you are invited to "serve" there you are very honoured indeed. You should most definitely give up your worldly belongings and go there to participate in God's free labour service. He's still resting you see, on his seventh day of creation so the little worker ant humans must keep things running for him down here on this measly wee planet, at least until he decides to come and wipe out most of humanity in something called Armageddon. I've mentioned it before, but Armageddon is basically the emotional control tool wielded over Jehovah's Witnesses to make sure they comply with any instruction the Governing Body dishes out. Examples are many and easily found if you visit their website. I'm not going to give them a free plug, instead what I will say is if you want to know more, please visit some of the many fabulous content creators and authors in the Recommended Reading section of this book who can summarise Watchtower and The Governing Body's corrupt policies far better than I ever could.

If you are a Jehovah's Witness you must do your best, no in fact you must go over and above and beyond your best to make sure you preach to as many people as possible that Armageddon is coming. If you don't do this then you will have blood guilt on your hands and you might not make it through to the other side yourself. God can be very strict about who he kills and who he spares. Take Sodom and Gomorrah for instance. He made sure he got Lot and his family out so he could destroy the entire city with fireballs from heaven, but Lot's wife took a backwards glance and then became a pillar of salt. Its human nature to glance at things. We're visual creatures. Can any of us really say with certainty we wouldn't have taken a sneaky peak to see what God was up to? I'm not sure I would be able to resist. I'm pretty nosey like. So Lot, having lost his home, all of his possessions and his wife, now has to live in a cave, get drunk every night and have sex with his daughters to ensure his family line continues after the destruction of all humanity in the nearby vicinity. These are the kind of Biblical events my Mum used to love telling me about while I was having my breakfast and trying to think about getting through the day ahead at School. She loved a good fireball fest did my Mum. In her mind, put there of course by the Governing body via the indoctrination and directives contained in their literature, she HAD to preach this to me to make sure I was fully aware of my lifestyle choices. If she told me enough about the fireballs in the past, and the ones soon to fall from the sky in the future, then there would be no blood on her hands, she had tried her best and completed her assignment.

When Covid suddenly hit in late 2019/early 2020 Angel suddenly became the predominant guiding voice in my mind reminding me of things Mum had said with such conviction and determination. Spewing forth scriptures I had been repeatedly made to read as a child which haunted me now as an adult. The first one which jumped straight into my mind was Luke 21:11 which in the New World Translation aka The Jehovah's Witness specific translation of the Bible reads as:

"There will be great earthquakes, and in one place after another food shortages and pestilences; and there will be fearful sights and from heaven great signs"

This scripture kept popping in and out of my head. It just would not go away.

Angel had been gnawing at me for a while with her concerns that maybe Mum had it right after all? Humanity did seem to be teetering on the brink of something big. Maybe the world was going to end soon and I had already used up all of my chances, if I wasn't careful my life of sin would catch up on me right as the door to salvation was closing. I would be left outside, weeping in the rain just as the people in the days of Noah's flood had done. Mum loved to tell me the story about how it was Jehovah who shut the door to the ark, so that everyone and everything outside it drowned. That never made any sense to me. It also terrified me as I couldn't swim and had a water phobia, Mum knew this one would really hit the spot in my impressionable young mind.

What sort of crazy power trip was God on though? He makes the fruit trees, says "eat what you want, oh except don't eat this one because if you do you'll be able to think and make decisions for yourself rather than blindly obeying" When Adam and Eve fail the test as it was inevitable they would, he chucks them out into the desert ordering their offspring to commit incest in order to populate the planet. Years later he goes on a mass murdering spree undoing everything he asked humans to achieve. He then feels regret and puts a rainbow in the clouds as if that's going to fix everything. Noah's offspring repopulate the planet again to epic proportions, then at an undisclosed time in the future, he plans once again to commit genocide, only this time using hailstones as big as footballs alongside the old faithful fireballs.

I never could get my head around how a "loving God" could do things like this. He seemed more like some kind of crazed egocentric maniac to me, but the way my Mum continually described Armageddon terrified me. At the same time as she was terrifying me with the fireballs and vultures coming to peck my eyes out after my fiery demise, she was dangling the carrot of salvation with her other hand. It's a classic JW mind control cult training technique. Scare your subject into submission then tempt them with a pretty picture to help them blot out the barbaric one they've just envisioned. If you can survive Armageddon and make sure you don't look back you get the lovely paradise with the pandas and as much fruit as you can eat for the rest of eternity.

I always liked fruit and pandas so I somehow manage to sidestep the fact God is a homicidal maniac, hell bent on periodically destroying his creations by telling myself if I make sure I'm not too late into the final "ark" I will manage to have it both ways. I can enjoy a "worldly" life of debauchery and then, right at the last minute I can repent, hop aboard and sail into the Paradise. I say this half-jokingly to Mum in one of our intense after school study sessions, I also tell her I'm struggling with the concept of lions suddenly having square teeth and eating grass. JW's teach that animals will all become placidly herbivorous after Armageddon which was something I never could get to grips with. I'm a child, but a well-educated one, I understand fully the concept of balance in nature. I'm a huge David Attenborough fan and love watching nature programs. I have books on my bookshelves written by him describing in great detail the way carnivores hunt and devour their prey. The balance of nature means if a species becomes too populated something natural will cull it back to the correct proportions if man doesn't step in and do the job. Maybe this was why years later I became a pest controller myself? It makes sense to me if the planet gets over populated something has to be done or our species will be on a self-destruct course. But as much as my rational mind tells me a human "cull" might make the earth a better place and I want to be a survivor, it seems so awful that's what has to happen to fix things. Surely God can come up with a better plan?

He designed and made everything and has no beginning or end - why can't he just find a more amicable solution, why does everything have to be death, violence and bloodshed? She tells me I shouldn't be reading those books anymore as scientists are tainted by Satan and write lies about evolution. I juggle David Attenborough and Mum in my mind trying to decide who's opinion I respect most. I tell her I'm not getting rid of them and besides she has a book about Atlantis which surely can't be scriptural? The next day it's in the bin. I go to fish it out as I wouldn't mind a read of it, she tells me to leave it where it is!

I tell her I'm struggling with a lot of the teachings and I think I'd rather just do my own thing until I see some real actual signs that all of this isn't just a whole load of baloney. Then and only then, I might take action. She gives me a chilling warning that God can read people's hearts and he is listening to our conversation right now. He won't let me into the paradise if that's my attitude. She tells me the time period were living in is like an hourglass where the sand is running out. The last little bit that falls will happen so suddenly and then that's it, out of time!

It's shocking really the things JW's teach their children, some of the graphic pictures in their children's books of people and animals drowning, or people running from the coming carnage of Armageddon are enough to give a kid traumatic nightmares never mind if the parent reading to them has a fireball fetish to go with the stories.

What's more shocking is that I reached a point in my adult life where I had just escaped from a high control, abusive relationship with a man and somehow Angel, my guiding voice at the time, thought it was a good idea to now jump into a similarly high control, abusive one with eight men from Brooklyn wanting to micromanage my life rather than just one from Belfast, but the moment that pandemic hit I think we all lost a wee bit of our sanity.

Sadly, it's often the case that abuse attracts abuse. In much the same way as a woman who witnesses her Father beat her Mother as a child might unwittingly enter into violent or abusive relationships as an adult, so many abuse sufferers run from one abusive situation straight into the next one. We want the opposite of what we choose, but were subconsciously drawn like a moth to a flame, to what feels familiar or "normal" despite it being the worst choice for us.

To add further madness to an already surreal situation I have Angel telling me "Look how happy your Sister is" There's no hobosexual waster men in her life making it a misery. She's been washed clean by the blood of the Lamb of God. She's got inner contentment and is happy and busy with loads of quality friends and uplifting social events. What have you got to show for your life so far? What have you ever done that has any meaning or purpose? She's always telling me how wonderful life is in "Jehovah's Service" I've never been a fan of serving anyone but I feel like there's this piece of the puzzle of life missing, maybe this is the thing which will fill it properly?

The "pestilences" kept churning around in my mind. I always said if I saw a sign all of this was real I would act on it. Was this the sign? What should I do? Was I already too late? JW's teach that there will be a time just before Armageddon called the Great Tribulation where everything will go crazy bonkers and people all across the globe will be in fear. This seemed to fit what was currently happening. A daily news feed full of death tolls, stark warnings, conspiracy theories, worried friends and neighbours, people having meltdowns over the tiniest of things. People fighting and jostling in supermarkets over the last multi-pack of toilet rolls! Everyone seemed so stressed and angry plus the unprecedented "pestilence" wreaking its havoc across the globe freaked me out. I felt anxious, struggled to sleep at night, had strange, scary apocalyptic dreams and generally felt very on edge. I was fortunate in that my job at the time allowed me to travel where others had to stay home so in general it was actually a good time for me, I was making lots of money and didn't feel the cabin fever most people were experiencing, but my childhood indoctrination was essentially ruining what could or should have been a wonderful time. The blue skies we had during those early spring months of lockdown were the clearest I've seen since the times as a child lying in the hay fields. I always took it that the "sign" in the sky would be something magnificent but what if it was just the fact we could see the sky again clearly due to all the air traffic being absent? I kept asking myself if someone from Jesus' day were alive today what would they consider to be "fearful sights" and signs in the sky? Would the mere sight of an aeroplane or the ISS terrify them? Quite possibly!

I hate an unsolved question, it rumbles round and round in my head until I start to feel nauseous. I need answers! "Ring your Sister, she will know what to do", Angel tells me soothingly. So I ring her and tell her my thoughts and ask her if there's much time left? Am I too late? Reassuringly she tells me no, the Governing

Body who are God's Mouthpiece on Earth
haven't yet announced the end of days, there's a
tiny bit of time left but If I'm sure about this,
really, really sure about it, we can have an
intensive Bible study to bring me up to speed on
what I've missed out on over the years.

Devil says what a load of hoo-hah you're not
seriously going to sign up for this shite are you?
Just turn off the News and enjoy the peace and
quiet on your daily walks 'cos everyone else is
so much of a rule obeyer they are all at home
day drinking in their gardens.

Angel says your whole life you have been
running and hiding from this, deep down you
know it's right, what have you got to lose by
delving a bit further to see if it's for you or not?

I have nothing to use as a defence for what I
did next other than childhood indoctrination
having a far stronger hold on me than I realised
but I go with Angel and decide to give this a go.
I will let myself tumble down this rabbit hole
and see just how far it goes. Best case scenario –
I get to live forever and not get any more grey
hairs, saggy bits or wrinkles. Worst case
scenario – it will be an interesting and character
building experience, a journey of

self-improvement, enlightenment and higher consciousness.

My Sister is ecstatic of course, she lets out a little squeal of excitement, she has always wanted to have a Bible study with me. So we set up a schedule online, as were not allowed to meet up due to the Lockdown protocol and we get stuck straight in.

In the early stages its quite interesting but we soon start to come across issues. I have questions, so many of them, she's struggling to cope with them all so other people must be brought in to help. I'd prefer it to just be me and her enjoying our time together but she tells me that's the rules, the Governing Body have rules about EVERYTHING and that's how we have to do it, so I say OK and wait to see what happens next. Lots of different women from her congregation come along to our study over the coming weeks. Men aren't allowed to come as that would be "inappropriate". Having previously lived a life of slutty debauchery I'm not allowed to be alone with any men even if it is online. The angels are always watching me and monitoring everything I do and I mustn't say or do anything that might stumble anyone.

For example I mustn't wear anything too low cut in case they look at my cleavage and start to lust after me. So it's women only!

They're all lovely of course and I make some new friends. She then tells me the next step is for me to attend the meetings. I'm not keen on this as I remember well being dragged to them as a youngster but she tells me this new online way of doing it is great! You don't have to leave your house and it won't be for long anyway, the end is just around the corner, almost in sight. Any day now we will see the start of the Great Tribulation and I'm in the right place to ensure a seat on the big bus of salvation. I must start to do my own personal study though in between our online study sessions and the twice weekly meetings. I must start taking in "Spiritual Food" which means I must watch videos of the Governing Body Members, dressed in their fancy suits, wearing their expensive watches and jewellery and telling me what I should and shouldn't be doing. One of the eight men in particular is like something out of a cartoon. He makes weird noises and pulls exaggerated faces as he talks. When I'm alone in private I can't stop laughing at how ridiculous he is and Devil says "Seriously? Are you actually going to take advice from this crazy dude? He looks like the long lost twin brother of that Doomsday Cult guy who made everyone drink coolade so they could catch a lift on a comet tail. What the FUCK!?!"

Angel tells me to keep going, I promised her I'd see where this path would take me so I need to at the very least see things through until we get into the paradise, which will be really, really soon. Goon Guy on the telly says so too, so it must be true. He widens his crazy eyes, contorts his big gurney face and says "We are living in the final part of the final part of the final part of the final part of the final part of the last days" I guess I don't have to stick it all out for long then. Not too many more videos to wade through until I get my wee wooden cabin in the woods where I can recreate the scene from Cinderella every morning by opening my windows and being joined by an endless stream of cute, friendly animals and birds.

I honestly think I was in some sort of deluded daydream writing this now, but I kept on with the study schedule and for a time it was bearable but then I was told that I wasn't allowed to study with my sister anymore. She now had to hand the study over to someone in Scotland. This meant once the lockdown ends I can go to the actual meetings, not virtual ones. Wait....what?? Hang on, I thought Armageddon was coming so we wouldn't ever have to go to actual meetings again as the time left is so short? I'm not keen on all this and Devil is starting to gnaw at me with his jibes about how I am being taken for a numpty with all of this nonsense. I should just say "Sorry Sis I've made a mistake I'm going back to my sinful life, hope you have a nice time at your Armageddon BBQ" But I don't listen to him, I will stick with the program for just now. Strong the indoctrination force in this one is! I made this promise to Angel to see what's at the very end of the rabbit hole, so I keep on going.

The new study lady is nice and we forge what I think is a friendship of sorts, she seems very sweet and caring and once again I make new friends. She tells me I'm doing really well I'm making spiritual progress and I'm well on the way to being a candidate for baptism. There's just a few things we need to iron out first though. I need to make sure I change my hair as its too "Worldly" and might cause "stumbling" amongst other ladies in the congregation. I tell her I like my haircut. It helps hide the greys. I never had a single grey hair until I met Mr Nasty. Now I have loads! When I wear it down you can't see how short some parts of it are and even when I wear it up I still look like a woman. Gender blurring is very bad in the JW religion they are very anti-gay and some of the Governing Body make ranty videos about men not being allowed to wear tight fitting trousers in case it turns them into a homosexual. Tight fitting trousers are designed by homosexuals, for homosexuals they rant, and JW's must be "No part of the World" so these drainpipe type suits are a big no go. Haircuts can be an issue with men too. If they spend too much effort on their hair they could fall into the "metro sexual" category and that's dangerous ground. And beards! Men aren't allowed to have beards. I can't see the logic in this as Jesus had one? Devil is whispering "Get out, Get your running shoes on and get outta there!" Nice new study lady sends me a photo of Miley Cyrus and tells me I can't have a haircut that emulates the "Spirit of the World" I say that there are Sisters in the congregation who have shorter hair than I do and look much less feminine. I name one in particular who is her friend and the conversation bombs like a lead balloon. I'm left to think about things and have to come to a decision by myself. We all have free will. The Loving, caring God Jehovah gave us the gift of it. We can either make choices of our own and die sinful, or do as were told and live forever in the Paradise. It's a multiple choice life and death question no one else can make for us. I decide I was due for a change anyway and had thought about growing it out as it's so hard to get a regular haircut during Covid so I'll grow it out. Devil says "if you're going to do it, do it for YOU not them". Angel is quietly watching the proceedings and saying nothing.

The rules come thicker and faster as the weeks go on. Baptism gets mentioned more and more. I'm not keen on this at all as I can't swim and have this silly water phobia plus there's something strange going on I can't put my finger on in the background making me want to just up and do a runner from all of this. Devil keeps saying "You do know this is all a big bunch of nonsense don't you? Why are you going along with it"?

I am invited to watch a baptism online with several of the people I've gotten to know over the last few months. It's difficult to watch, one of the ladies seems to have difficulty when the Brother doing the baptism tries to bend her over backwards so she ends up getting dunked more than once and it begins to look more like a drowning than a dedication. I watch through my fingers in much the same way as I do when the Bungling Buffoon of the Governing Body comes on to speak. Everything about him grates on me like nails down a blackboard. I can't watch his videos without laughing so every time we have to watch one in our online studies or meetings I switch my camera off so nobody can see or hear me guffawing with laughter. They are all sitting watching him with adoration and respect like rows of nodding dogs on the parcel shelf of a car. The gnawing feeling just won't go away now it's getting worse every week.

I'm being pushed to join the field ministry group. This makes my Mum and Sister so happy. They coo over me like a child and talk about how well I'm doing. I should by now know the signs of love bombing but when it's your family doing it, it's much easier to excuse. We're being told we must write letters. It's the new and improved door knocking. Were told its better than door knocking because if you send a hand written letter it might touch someone's heart who wouldn't normally open the door. We don't have to worry about spelling or proper names or even addressing it correctly, because the angels are up there guiding everything we do to make sure it all goes perfectly. Everyone in the world must get a letter telling them about Jehovah because the end can't come until everyone has been warned.

I join in with this campaign which at first seems fine until all the additional rules and regulations get tacked on. You can't just sit and write your letters at home. Well, you can... but that wouldn't be very good for you spiritually, you're much better to join in with a group of other people to write them online so you can get close to these people. They will be your new spiritual family to replace the worldly one you leave behind. Except I've no intentions of leaving anyone behind! My friends are my friends no matter what. They have been there for me through thick and thin. I'm not going to desert them just because some guy in a shirt and tie tells me they are "bad association". More and more doubts start to pop up about all of this stuff and Devil tells me to pretend I've written the letters but actually not write anything at all. He argues a very good point that if the angels really are directing things then all we have to do is write them and pop the blank envelopes in the post-box, they will do the rest. He's pretty persistent and I start holding my clipboard and pen during the meetings pretending to write but actually I'm just doodling.

The Baptism word keeps coming up again and again and eventually the lovely sister breaks it to me that actually all of this study and meetings have just been a preparation. What's really needed is for me to make a dedication to God and get baptised because only baptised Witnesses will survive during Armageddon. I can't find this anywhere in the Bible and the scriptures they give me don't seem to add up. I'm also told I must give up hunting and shooting because these things make me a "lover of violence". What an amusing thought considering were dealing with a "loving God" who thinks nothing of having animals killed so he can smell the pleasing aroma of their sacrificial smoke or wiping out millions of innocent creatures in a deluge.

I'm starting to think Devil has a point about this being baloney. There's also the masturbation thing too. I don't do it much these days as I seem to have completely lost my mojo and sex drive since having my operation and all the stuff that happened with my ex, sex is the last thing on my mind, but on the rare occasions I do fancy a feel it's just not the same now I've had the vision planted in my mind of Jesus, his Dad and myriads of angels watching me do it! I try to do it furtively under the covers in the dark but remember that they see everything.

A life with boring hair, ankle length skirts and endless rules looms in front of me. No shooting, no masturbation, I must be dunked deep in the pool to make sure the water goes right through one ear, cleanses all the dirty thoughts, squirts out of the other ear, shaking Devil off my shoulder for good, and then I will emerge, the newly cleansed and purified me. I must send a tithe of my wage to Watchtower and If I do ever regain any frisky feelings, which study lady assures me I will, because Satan is always roving about looking for ways to corrupt us with our weaknesses, I can only choose a husband from the dreggish pool of men in the congregation. Or wait until convention season which is the unofficial place JW's go to look for other equally depressed single JW's. This is all creepy and wrong. I'm getting some of this

"New light" they keep talking about and I don't like the look of the path it's illuminating in front of me.

Things come to a head when the baptism thing is really being pushed at me one day. I have several sisters all cooing at me saying how well I'm doing and if I just get baptised everything will be brilliant. Baptism is just the beginning, the gateway that opens up fabulous new opportunities like serving where the greed is greater, building real estate properties free of charge for Watchtower or perhaps even marrying an Elder and being allowed to iron his shirts and ties for the meetings. I tell my study lady I need to make sure I am 100% sure about what I would be signing my life up to first. I narrowly escaped baptism as a child, I would be a fool to rush into it now as an adult. The vast majority of JW's are born into the religion, pressured into baptism by their keen parents and trapped into this strict way of life. The rare occasions adults are baptised, it's usually because they are desperately looking to fill some form of void in their lives. I fully recognise that I fit the latter category and need to be really sure this is for me. I want to do some research. The aghast "Ooooohs" are audible. I must be very careful, Satan has set up a whole world of vicious apostate lies out there so I must ONLY research from the JW website and publications. If I look anywhere else for guidance, I will surely be led astray and all my progress I've made these last few months will have been in vain.

Around about this time, a Governing Body video appears in which one of them states that in the paradise we will have "Paradise Cities" and we might end up being assigned to Paradise Jobs which we might not like. We might prefer our log cabin in the woods, having a fruit breakfast while playing with our pet panda, but just as we have to be faithful to what the Watchtower men tell us to do just now in this wicked 'ol system, we will have to be obedient in the new system too.

Well this sucks! This has all been a big lie hasn't it? Devil nods furiously.

I've seen this guy before in other videos, he sometimes has a pointy stick he uses to tap his visual aids for emphasis. He reminds me of a strict school teacher. That long cane is totally there to hit you with if you misbehave during class or don't grasp the lesson. There are lots of other videos saying we must all be obedient to the Governing Body even if they tell us we should do things which might go against reason or common sense.

I look around at the sea of faces on screen and don't see one single person who looks concerned about this. I search their faces for any sign of life and all I see are empty eyes, fake smiles and steadily bobbing heads. So this is how it is then? what if the Governing Body tell you to jump? Do you ask how high?

I have a mini flashback to the film the Matrix where Neo wakes up and I feel like my plug has been unceremoniously yanked from the socket in the back of my head. I tell myself it was only hanging there by a thread, these poor buggers here are so plugged in they would need surgical intervention to cut them loose.

I now feel like I want to jam on the handbrake and get off the big salvation bus. I don't want to live in a city, paradise or any other kind. I'm a country girl through and through. I also can have a deadbeat job I hate in this system, God knows I've already had plenty of those I don't need to wait 'til after the fireball fest to have Director Dave here tell me which toilets I'm going to be cleaning. I don't want to be part of the collective "We" herded into submission by pointy stick man or given our rules by a guy who looks like he stepped through a Warner Bros Looney Tune circle. I remember a saying I once heard that if something is the truth then it will stand up to scrutiny. I can't remember whether I read this in the Bible itself or whether it was a Mark Twain quote but it grabs me hard. The scriptures tell you to examine something to see if it's the truth. If I'm being warned only to look at one side of the evidence surely it's not a fair trial?

Devil urges me "Fuck them, you go look at whatever you want to 'til you find the answers you need!"

So I do.

Chapter 20

Hateful ~~Eight, Ten,~~ Nine

The moment I grant myself permission to look at the alternative narrative to the one portrayed on the JW website, my great and life changing Apocapiphany begins. It's as though the floodgates have opened and I'm hit with a deluge of information, almost too much to take in at once. The first video I come across is a rather striking chap called Lloyd Evans. He's filming from inside some sort of massive JW library, rows upon rows of Witness Books line the shelves behind him, but I soon see from his content he's most definitely not a JW. I am immediately drawn though to his sharp wit, factual evidence and he's also a Star Wars geek which seals the deal. I do find myself feeling a strange sense of guilt though, as my finger hovers over the subscribe button, as if I'm Eve herself sampling the forbidden fruit. Each time he says something mocking the Governing Body, especially certain members, I guffaw loudly with laughter and think he's got it spot on with his observations, he even has some of their voices and mannerisms to a T.

Each time I laugh I then feel guilty and it's a while before I'm able to watch some of his videos from start to finish in their entirety. I've seen the JW propaganda telling JW's they mustn't follow suspicious links or be suckered in by evil apostate lies. This guy doesn't seem like a liar he's an ex-Elder and is delivering more sensible talks than any I've ever seen come from the Platform. Still, I exercise caution and only watch snippets here and there, if I agree with too much of what he says or laugh too much then I'm not showing a Christian spirit but a rebellious one and I'm in deep trouble as far as surviving Armageddon goes. That's if I even believe in all that anymore? I'm not sure what I believe but I'm determined to get to the bottom of all of this to find out.

One day whilst guiltily surfing his videos, a suggestion pops up on the right hand side of my screen. Its entitled Australian Royal Commission and has tags relating to child abuse. I click and begin watching. What I see over the next couple of hours has me absolutely glued to the screen. The man conducting the enquiry is very succinct and well versed on JW policies. When he questions them I feel like I'm secretly rooting for him, he has them tied in knots. The final nail in the coffin comes when Jibba Jabba Geoff one of the Governing Body members takes the stand. I call him this because a lot comes out of his mouth but not much of it makes sense. He swears on the Bible and then proceeds to tell lies in his testimony! I have heard JW's talking about Spiritual/Scriptural Warfare but now I'm actually seeing it in action in a courtroom. Jesus taught that we should be truthful, JW's call their religion "The Truth" because of this command and yet here's one of their leaders telling outright blatant lies. Scriptural Warfare, along with Governing Body is a man made term, found nowhere in the Bible. It means you are allowed to tell lies if you want or need to, to get yourself out of a sticky situation regarding doctrine or anything else you don't want to answer truthfully.

The Governing Body are at the top of the Watchtower chain of command and they make (and break) the rules, which are then passed down to the Elders and Circuit Overseers, who in turn then enforce them on the congregation members. Here I am not even halfway through this video and I can plainly see the rot from the top down. As I continue to watch I find out about the secret database Watchtower keep on child sex abuse perpetrators and immediately I'm transported back to that fateful day as a child when the Elders came to visit and cover over what my Dad had done! I wonder what notes they scrawled during and after this meeting and where they were filed? My nerves are jangling now and I feel angry and restless, this is not right! I'm just one person who had this bad experience, my Dad getting off Scot free with what he did pales in comparison with what others have had to endure, but I always thought it was an isolated incident. Now I'm discovering there are thousands of other cases and that's just from this one video alone covering Australia. I wonder what the UK results are? Or the Worldwide ones? JW's are active in every country across the globe.

The revelations now come thick and fast. I feel like I've been under a rock for years, how did I not know about this? This has been going on for years and on a shocking scale! Each time there is an allegation of child abuse, if the "Two Witness" policy isn't in place, it gets filed away in a cabinet somewhere and nothing gets done about it! As if a child molester is going to rape or assault children when there's anyone else present! Often the only time someone gets outed as being an abuser and brought to justice is when someone is brave enough to blow the whistle and go to the "Secular Authorities" themselves, risking disfellowshipping and shunning from their family and friends in the process. What I read and watch over the next few days absolutely disgusts me to the core. This is wrong, so wrong! Something needs to be done about this. I watch testimonies and read news articles from brave survivors who spoke out about what happened to them. I cry with them, and for them as I listen to their traumatic experiences. All of them have suffered far worse than me, some children were systematically abused for years and had to face their abuser on a weekly basis at the meetings, listening to them giving talks counselling others about their conduct, whilst being completely shielded and above the law regarding their own behaviour!

I feel sick to my stomach. My study conductor senses something is wrong. My spiritual progress seems to have plateaued or possibly even regressed, is there something wrong? Do I want to talk about it?

Do I ever, I feel like I want to scream from the rooftops "I can't believe this is happening and on such a scale!" but I must exercise caution for fear of my own family shunning me. My Mum and Sister will turn their backs on me if they think I've been tainted by apostates. I was estranged from my Mother for many years in my teens and twenties and now that she's getting elderly I don't want to lose that relationship that I have managed to rebuild with her.

So I tread carefully, I stick as close to the truth as I can without giving too much away. I want to extricate myself from the cultish mess I've come precariously close to dedicating the remainder of my life to. I tell her I had a traumatic childhood event and that when it occurred the Elders covered it up. I tell her I can't sign my life, as pathetic as it's been so far, up to something until I know all of the facts about everything from the top to the bottom, inside and out. I need to go off and do some further research and think deeply about things. I stop my study and no longer attend the meetings. She's upset and issues me with cautionary tales about going off and looking at apostate material, but the fact is I've already looked, I've seen, believed and now cant unsee it or act as though everything's OK.

276

During one of my research missions I discover that there's a "secret Elder's manual" which ordinary JW's are not allowed to read. Women are most definitely NOT allowed to touch it let alone read it. Red flag to a bull, the first thing I do is download a copy from a Watchtower leaks page and go straight to the chapter about child abuse and how Elders are to deal with it. It's probably one of the most lengthy chapters in the book, clearly because they have such a massive issue with it, enough to easily rival if not surpass other religious organisations such as the Catholic Church.

I feel so sick that this is happening, in plain sight, yet hidden from, all the average rank and file members of the religion. In many cases even if someone is found guilty of child abuse, the worst that might happen is they are made to stand down as an Elder or whatever position they hold and are given a warning. That's it! If they "repent" and say sorry then in a few years' time the whole thing might blow over as though it never happened. All the while their abuse victim(s) are struggling to cope with life on a day to day basis. I don't know the exact figures but I suspect the death toll from suicide of JW's subjected to abuse which was never pursued

276

through the proper legal justice systems will be high, far higher than it should be. If just one person takes their own life because of evils inflicted on them by purported Christians who should know better, then it's one too many!

My study conductor tells me she doesn't feel equipped to cope with my doubts and that I should speak to the Elders. As nice as they all are, I firmly say "No thanks". They are just the monkeys following the chain of command, the organ grinders are sitting in Brooklyn making up the rules, hiding all the secret database files, even going as far as to refuse to release them to authorities and courts, preferring instead to pay huge sums of money or settle with child abuse victims out of court. All of these huge sums of money are coming out of the pockets of essentially mild mannered, decent, working class people who are regularly encouraged by means of evangelising videos to donate every spare penny they have to the "Worldwide Work"

It makes me sick to the core to think my Mum and Sister have direct debits set up so their money goes to fund this sort of abysmal disgrace.

I tell her straight, along with my sister that I intend to cut out the middle men and go straight to the guys at the top who are making these appalling rules and ask first of all why? Second of all what, if anything do they plan to do in the future to rectify this and make sure their policies for handling child abuse going forwards don't result in the same mistakes being made and countless children being abused.

I'm told that whilst it's my right to do this, I'm breaking protocol by doing so as there's a structured hierarchy with unbaptised women and children being firmly at the very bottom of the pecking order. To write to the Governing Body in the U.S, bypassing the UK branch entirely with all its tiers of men in between, how shocking for a woman to do this. The Apostle Paul was very fond of telling people in his sermons that women should be silent. I was making myself heard! My first official act of rebellion since I began my study. I do it anyway and a copy of the letter I finally received from them after three months is enclosed in the addendum of this book. You can read it for yourself and see if you think it satisfactorily answers the questions I raised. Personally, nothing will satisfy me until their policies are changed to fully protect children.

Around this time, a video is made by one of the "Hateful Eight" which I've come to learn through my new apostate friends is the colourful euphemism given to the Governing Body. How well it fits them! This particular guy, we shall call him Tight Pants Tony since he has a hatred for men wearing anything more fashionable than beige baggy chinos, tells us all in no uncertain terms that the policies that govern JW life will NEVER be changed.

Well how about that? Because I distinctly remember watching one of the other Hateful Eight members stating under oath that they might consider changing and improving the status quo to make reporting to the authorities mandatory and also women could be involved in judicial committees as well as men.

That's the old Scriptural warfare in action again. I toy with the idea of writing them another letter, but decide they are not worth the paper and the postage to wait another 3 months to read more pacifying lies. I'm now subscribed to lots of ex JW channels, the ones I found most helpful and inspiring, or funny and light hearted

I have included in the recommended reading section. I have full respect for these content creators as they helped me "Wake Up" from the clutches of the PIMI army, to PIMO and then finally, the most liberating state of all : POMO.

Going POMO isn't a journey to be taken lightly, it's important to add. If you are baptised and dedicated and unrepentantly wake up from your cult slumber, you will almost certainly lose your believing family and friends who will shun you. There will be a talk delivered at your local Kingdom Hall to warn others of your fateful path and they must be careful not to follow in your doomed footsteps. They won't name you outright but everyone in the congregation will nod and whisper and gossip, even though gossiping is considered a sin. Trust me they will ALL know who that warning talk is all about.

You may feel utterly depressed and dejected as I did when you realise the entire belief system you had, or rather had drummed into you from childhood was all a lie. One aimed at fear mongering you into a set of behaviours designed to pacify a God who is neither loving, caring nor compassionate. A flawed belief system that makes you reject anything "Satan's

World" might have to offer in the way of friendships, relationships, music, hobbies, careers or happiness. It's drummed in to children from the cradle upwards that to seek your own pleasure and happiness in life is wrong, you must put God first and wait and delay, anything offered in this life is only temporary, the real reward comes in the future, the pandas and the banquet tables full of food where nobody ever gets sick or sad.

To realise this was all a big dupe to get you to perform free labour for Watchtower an American real estate company or donate your hard earned money to them, or both, can be as depressing and humiliating as finding out your partner was leading a double life. You feel stupid, which was something I was beginning to feel on a very regular basis.

I watch and read everything I can about the real JW history, the one they like to white wash or tell parts of but not others. I sit up until the wee small hours devouring everything I can, soaking it up like a sponge. I don't think I can "fade" which is the slow, steady exit from the cult many ex JW's have to carefully plan and execute. I'm too much of a straight talker for that so my exit will be rather more with a bang. At this point I would like to say that I completely disagree with the movement where ex JW activists go on Kingdom Hall and Memorial "crashing" crusades. I think this is counterproductive to the cause and just feeds into the whole JW persecution propaganda. For every say 100 people in a Kingdom Hall which has a meeting disrupted, only a very small percentage might be interested in secretly listening to what the crashers have to say. The bulk of the members are so brain washed to close their ears to any source outside of Watchtower, it actually flips a "mute" switch in their minds so they can't listen, even if they wanted to. It plays right into their narrative and enables them to go "Look, see! We told you about the angry apostates and look what they're doing now!"

Also, for the most part, the little people at the bottom really are the meek of the earth that Jesus spoke about. Most of them are genuine, mild mannered, law abiding, decent humans who just happen to be caught in a mind control cult. They should invoke our empathy not rage. They are trapped and held hostage by the invisible fence inside their mind. The kindest thing you can do for a PIMI JW is to simply be there for them if they wake up and help them through it until they are fully POMO.

It's well worth noting that this chapter was originally named "Hateful Eight" but shortly before I finished this book, an almost unprecedented event occurred and two new virtually unknown members of the Governing Body were appointed taking the numbers up to ten. A short while later it was announced that Tight Pants Tony was no longer a Governing Body member! So Eight becomes ten, becomes nine.

Has Tony been ejected in some kind of Spiritual coup?

Amidst much speculation we don't currently have a clear cut reason for this. All we can do is await further enlightenment. The Governing Body is fond of dishing out "New Light" when it concerns changing doctrinal understanding to suit their narrative or add further burdensome rules to an already super strict cult, but are much less enthusiastic when it comes to giving out information on paedophiles contained within their ranks or announcing their financial statements.

The Ex JW community is alive with gossip and speculation and the general consensus is that something big has gone down, but it'll likely take a serious amount of insider whistle blowing before we get to know what's really happened.

Alcohol abuse, child sex abuse cover ups and arguments over doctrinal matters are all offered as potential reasons for his removal but one thing's for sure, this is the biggest shake up that's happened within the top echelon of the Watchtower Society since the 1980s when Raymond Franz was removed. I think I speak for most ex JW's when I say his amazing book "Crisis of Conscience" is a must have for any apostate book shelf. If you are PIMI or PIMO or simply having doubts, the establishment will tell you not to read this book under any circumstances, in fact mere ownership or proof of reading of it can be enough to get you in the disfellowshipping recycle bin faster than Elijah running from Jezebel.

In time we might get a clearer picture of what happened, some "New Light" on the old dictator, but until then I am just so pleased I found this new, refreshing community, it wasn't an easy ride to get here but now that I am I feel a sense of purpose I never got the entire 2 years I spent studying the Bible as an adult or the many I spent being verbally bashed with it as a child.

I'm glad to be free as the next big life adventure feels to be just around the corner, unlike Armageddon which is dragging its heels well over 100 years in! Activism appeals to me and my new research project has become finding ways to provoke rational thought and gently wake up others still in the religion, whilst at the same time trying to raise awareness to everyone outside it about what's happening. I may not be able to do much but if anything I do from now on helps others or moves the wheels of progress towards change then it's better than sitting idle. JW's love to talk about Jehovah's celestial chariot which is always moving forwards and has wheels made of eyes. Those eyes must surely see all the awful things being done under the cover of his name so if he's not going to do anything about it, it's down to us.

Chapter 21

Horny Part III

Spoiler Alert : Come on.....you know the script by now....

Having finally shaken myself free from the unnerving grip of my childhood indoctrination (Thanks again Mum!) and my very close shave with the Watchtower society in adulthood, I now decide its time I really did some work on myself. I don't regret my time spent investigating this corrupt and coercive institution as the benefits of it far outweigh the downside. I find that learning about Christianity in general has had a positive effect on me. I'm far more empathetic, caring about the effect of my words and actions on others and I'm determined to use every day I'm alive to make a positive impact on people's lives, even if only in the smallest ways like a smile or a "Well done". I always felt that Jesus, whether a real person who actually came to Earth to sacrifice his life or a fictional character, was someone worth listening to. He certainly left a good model for humanity to follow. If more people in the world lived in harmony with his teachings we would see a lot less war, greed,

corruption, poverty and crime. So I definitely don't regret my time spent learning about him. I want to try to emulate his charitable qualities and honesty at all costs.

Most of all I want to be kinder to people around me, and perhaps most importantly to myself. I am my own worst critic, I regularly beat myself up internally, feeling deeply ashamed of the wrong turns I've taken and appalling choices I've made. One of the first steps I must take on this new path to becoming my very best authentic self is to be a bit kinder to myself when thinking in the past tense. Writing this book has not been easy and at times I've cringed so much at how stupid, gullible, misled, selfish and generally idiotic I have been. All of these roads led me to where I am right now though, so even if I could change any one of them, perhaps I wouldn't really want to. I sometimes feel like I'm torn in different directions not knowing the wisest way to turn, so I try hard to listen to my inner voice and make it the loudest influence over me, rather than giving any air time to Angel and Devil anymore. They are two opposing extremes and often the right path lies somewhere milder in between.

I also feel that my insider knowledge and experience of this organisation, although it's nothing in comparison to some of the experience people have at higher levels such as Bethel etc, puts me in a position to be able to do something proactive to help others. I've always enjoyed writing and I read several books by ex JW authors which really set my inspirational fire alight, but at the moment I'm just toying with the idea and nothing's giving me the burst of courage to get the ball rolling. The idea of writing even just an article lingers there in the background of my mind, aching for a catalyst to speed things up.

It's summer time and covid restrictions are now finally beginning to lift, so I venture out to a local event where I meet up with some friends I haven't seen for ages. My "Worldly" people I refused to abandon, and it feels so nice to see them all and give each other hugs and have a good old catch up. Covid has been doing the rounds though and never really went away, so the village fete ends up being a super spreader event and after 2 years of successfully dodging Covid, I come down with it and it hits me hard.

I'm immediately struck with how this doesn't feel like a normal flu or cold. My throat feels as though I've swallowed shards of glass, my ears feel full like I have cotton wool stuffed in them and there's a really horrible chemical taste in my mouth and back of my nose, a bit like the fumes from gloss paint. It feels like something man made rather than something natural if that makes any sense. I know a few people who Covid hit very badly who ended up with long covid and a couple of people who died, so I do panic a bit as I feel the fever gripping hold of me. At the same time as I'm panicking I also feel a strange feeling I've not felt in a long time. I'm as horny as hell!

It doesn't make any sense to me as I lie in bed feeling feverish and thoroughly sorry for myself, but all I want to do, to quote Watchtower one final time, is "manipulate my genitals" until I reach orgasm. Mr Man pops into my head which surprises me. Despite the fact Mr Nasty was obsessed with the idea I still thought about, dreamt about and met up with him behind his back, even though I never did any of those things, this is actually the first time in well over ten years he has entered my head space. Probably because up until now he's still the best sex I ever had so my covid crazed mind is drawing on its cheapest source for quick thrills. I have flashbacks to 20 years ago when we used to ravage each other and as I lie there feeling like I'm dying from this horrible virus, I also have the best orgasm I've had in I don't know how long. Fuck the angels, they can watch if they like, I don't care!

Over the next few days I alternate in and out of fever, delirium, horniness and restless sleep. Getting up only to use the toilet and take the dogs along to the woods, where I stand aching all over wishing they would hurry up and do their business so I can get back to my warm, cosy bed.

I'm going to blame Devil for this, I join a dating site and immediately I'm bombarded with messages from an assortment of men. I'm pleasantly surprised, I don't think I'm anything special but I do think I'm somewhat attractive and quirky, hopefully standing out from the crowd. Straight away there are a couple of main contenders. One man seems really nice, we have some great chats back and forth over the next few days and he sends me some sweet messages to cheer me up. I feel quite triumphant inside that my ex didn't manage to break my spirit entirely. He called me fat, lazy, stupid and boring so many times I had started to reluctantly believe him. He had an indoctrination all of his own which served the purpose of making me into a submissive slave to his own self-hatred. Projecting his thoughts about himself onto me to make him feel better. Fucked up is what that is. Come to think of it he would have made a great Elder wouldn't he? Just the right sort of disposition. Now, suddenly there seems to be an endless sea of men who find me quite the opposite, attractive, interesting and intelligent. I'm no fool though my time served on the sex chat lines along with my many dating disasters in the past have taught me plenty.

I know the drill now, older and wiser, my finger is poised above my block button at all times.

The old, ugly men outside of my age range who begin with "Hi Beautiful" or "What's a gorgeous girl like you doing on a site like this"? I blitz them immediately into the bin where they belong. I have my parameters firmly set, but you always get a steady stream of misfits and chancers who will try to sneak through your filters. I may be looking for a 45 – 55 year old 6ft plus man with dark hair and a good sense of humour, but you can bet your boots Barry, 75 and 5 foot 4 from Wales will want to strike up a chat about how he thinks we are soulmates. Or Carl, 26 and living in his parents' box room, thinks I look like a "hot MILF" even though I don't have any children, and do I fancy meeting up with him for "Sum NSA fun" These pond scum aren't even worth a reply, in the bin they go. I swipe no so many times the dating site tells me there are no more matches within a hundred mile radius and I should consider Barry from Cardiff as he's really keen.

I chat some more with the first man, who soon begins to annoy me. These days, after everything I've been through, I don't suffer fools or timewasters gladly. It's been a few weeks now and a pattern is emerging. He chats away for a few messages then vanishes. Sometimes for days on end. Then reappears like there haven't been days in between our last chat. Many girls would message in between but I know better than that, if a man wants you he wants you, you'll know all about it!

Yes, if he wants you he could also be a love bomber like my ex Mr Nasty, but I like to think I can spot those red flags since I'm so well acquainted with them now. It's taken me almost half a century but I got there in the end, I now feel like I can listen to my gut when its telling me something isn't quite right. I decide to write him off if he doesn't ask me out within the next week, which is being liberal because I think this man has no plans to ever ask me out if I'm being real with myself. The week comes and goes with nothing to show for it, other than a bloke who wants me to drive almost 3 hours to visit him just because I commented he had a nice camper van, and a guy in his 50's who turns out to be a militant vegan and gets upset when I tell him I enjoy countryside pursuits.

He doesn't ask me on a date so I strike a line through him and I decide to swap numbers with another man who's been messaging a fair bit and seems like a good prospect. He sounds nice on the phone and we have a lot in common, but he's going on holiday with his mate for a week so we can't meet until then. That's fine I say and leave him be, thinking "Yeah, Yeah" I'm such a sceptic now. But he messages me every day while he's away and shows me photos of his trip so maybe there actually are honest men still out there? I'm not convinced but I agree to meet up with him when he returns from his holiday. About halfway through his trip a guy I like the look of more pops up and seems keen to chat. He stands out from the sea of faces as he has clothes on in his photos, he's not flexing at the gym, not lying in bed topless looking like his other hand is busy and unlike so many men out there, he is smiling in his photos. If there was one piece of advice I would give to anyone using dating apps, male or female it would be to smile a bit more! It makes you look more genuine, approachable and less of a poser. Plus it lets a potential date see that you have teeth! I have been duped into going on a date once before with a toothless guy, once bitten twice shy, pardon the pun!

We chat back and forth and already I like the look and sound of him more than the other chap, but as my friend Mandy reminds me, men love to run strings of multiple women alongside each other, date them all and then pick the one they like best. She's excited for me to have two contenders as she's been on the apps for a while and isn't having any luck. She insists I absolutely MUST date them both, report back to her then pick the best one, it's my duty. Don't hate the player, just play the game she tells me. Things seem to have really gathered pace since the last time I tried online dating but I decide she's right. Nothing like a bit of healthy competition so I agree to a date with Mr Awesome, I'm going to call him that because as hard as I've tried I can't find any faults with him so far. I know I probably will down the line, but for just now I'm enjoying the feeling of chatting with and looking forward to getting to know someone who I just click with. I feel nervous and fluttery about meeting him even though we've only spoken a couple of times on the phone and exchanged a few photos. I don't get the same feeling with the other chap at all. I'm very take it or leave it where he's concerned.

Date night comes around and I'm so nervous, it's like being back in my twenties again. In more ways than one, as Covid has given me some sort of strange immune system boost and I'm now feeling the best I've felt in years. I have lost a stone in weight due to having no appetite, I'm an insomniac only sleeping around 5 hours a night on a good night and I'm just generally buzzing with life and brimming with ideas. I feel good about myself for the first time in a long time and I want someone to share this exciting feeling with. Even if he only turns out to be Mr Right for Right Now, I feel hopeful that good things are on the horizon for me. If not him, then someone else, someone better. I'm not fat, not ugly, not lazy, not stupid and certainly not dull so the world is my oyster. I'm going to strike while the irons hot.

I feel sick though as I get ready for my first meeting with Mr Awesome. I run back and forth to the loo and piddle with nervous excitement like a puppy. What if his photos are out of date, or he smells, or he has rubbish banter? What if he's an axe murderer? Mandy has my back, I tell her where and when we're meeting and if she doesn't hear from me she will sound the alert.

The minute he steps out of his car to greet me I am pleasantly surprised. He's exactly as he described himself which in itself is a rare thing on dating apps and if anything he's actually nicer looking than his photos.

We chat for ages about all sorts and I feel both comfortable with him and uncomfortable about my thought processes in equal measures. I want to kiss him really badly, Devil is saying "Do it, do it, do it" you know the score with him by now.

Angel is saying play it cool, aloof and coy, don't stare at him like a predatory lioness waiting to devour her next antelope, be cautious, men are mostly arseholes and you've been hurt enough. I play Angel's tactic but as the date comes to a close he asks if he can kiss me so we do. It's a good kiss! Sends tingles to all the right places. It's nice to be asked too, feels very old fashioned and gentlemanly. I don't know why but when he asks me my weekend plans I blurt out that I have another date. He looks a bit taken aback but I keep telling myself he is probably dating scores of other women, he's a good looking guy after all.

He tells me he prefers to date one woman at a time and isn't seeing anyone else just now and I think to myself this is either the best line ever or he is a unicorn of some kind.

My date with the other man comes around a few days later and I start to feel a bit bad and wonder if I should cancel, but Mandy soon puts me back on track telling me men do this sort of stuff to us women all the time. I need to evaluate my options. I have a scary moment where a man pulls up in the same type of car as the one he told me he is driving. He gets out and he's at least 60, has a huge big beer belly and is wearing baggy shorts and flip flops. He does a big yawny stretch and I turn my key in my engine ready to drive off, but luckily it's not him! A few moments later my actual date pulls up and gets out. His clothing isn't a huge improvement on the other man, but at least he actually looks somewhat like his photos, although its immediately obvious some of them were taken a while ago. He definitely looks chubbier and greyer. I've heard it said you form an impression of someone within the first few seconds of meeting them, I think it happened much faster than that. I knew immediately he was not for me. But we exchange pleasantries and a bit of small talk before I make my excuses and drive home. We even manage to have a laugh about the other man and how I very nearly didn't meet him at all! I don't see the point in giving anyone false hope though so it's a no from me. Besides, I want to see Mr Awesome again, the sooner the better. I've had a nice glow in my loins since our passionate kiss the other night and I'm looking forward to getting to know him in more ways than one.

The future looks bright for the first time in a long time.

Chapter 22

Happily Ever After?

It's summertime and I'm a few months into a new, exciting relationship with Mr Awesome. He hasn't put a foot wrong so far, he looks great, smells great, makes me feel good about myself, is good fun, interesting to talk to on any subject and he's fantastic in bed. I've deliberately left that until last so you don't think I'm shallow but oh my goodness the things he does to me hit secret spots I didn't know I had!

It's not all plain sailing though. The self-sabotaging, cyclic negative thought Gremlins dominate a lot of my head space.

"What if he's just lying to you about everything and it's all a big scam just like your ex"?

"What if he doesn't really like you he's just playing along for sex, boredom or any of the other reasons men string women along"?

"What if he's going to break your heart? Do you even have one left after everything that's happened"?

Angel reasons that he really does seem to genuinely care for me and he's done nothing so far to warrant this level of scrutiny. There comes a point where we have to let the past go and take that leap of faith. She's been wrong before so my trust in her is flawed, but I do hope she's right about this, if nothing else.

Devil says "Think of all the great sex you'll miss out on if you don't keep seeing him. Lots of sexy, sexual, sex." He really does have a one track mind, but also a valid point. I throb incessantly every time I think about meeting up with him and we have the most amazing chats about sexy stuff when were together and apart. The honeymoon period is just the best isn't it!

I decide to get therapy to help me deal with all of this because sometimes it feels like it's too much for one person to carry around. I want to have a nice, easy, pleasant relationship with this man, and not feel like I'm lugging a huge suitcase full of drama around with me everywhere I go.

One morning I wake up and Bam! I've had another one of my prophetic dreams. They don't happen often, so I recognise them the minute I wake from them. The dream itself is a very simple one, I see a book on someone's coffee table, I've no idea who's coffee table as that's the wonderful way dreams work, but there it is. It's drawing me to it like a magnet. It has a very distinctive cover and I want to open it up and begin reading. I turn the cover and go to the first page, reading the chapter list, then to the next page, but its blank. Then I wake up. How frustrating!

My morning routine always consists of walking the dogs before work, mulling things over while my mind is at its freshest, and trying my best to beat back the grouchy gremlins and their intrusive thoughts so I can enjoy my day as much as possible. All I can think about today is this Bloody Book!

I decide to Google it to see if I've seen this book before and it's just my subconscious showing me something I hadn't previously paid enough attention to. I recently finished reading a wonderful book by an ex JW author which I loved, I read it in one afternoon sitting on my sun lounger and it made me feel brave enough to perhaps tell my story too? There's nothing on Google the book does not exist.

This should be the end of it, but it's not and the book niggles away at me all day. Later that day, while giving the dogs their afternoon walk it comes to me, clearly and succinctly, that this is MY book. I don't know why or how I just know that it doesn't exist yet because I haven't written it. The micro second the thought enters my head it feels so right, I know that's the answer and I feel chuffed to bits. I begin writing it a few days later on a camping trip at the beach, with the sun setting across the sea in front of me, barefoot on my sun lounger with sand between my toes, a cold beer on one side of me and a nicely smoking firepit on the other. My little lapdog laid across me, looking out at the waves contentedly, rising and falling gently as I tap away like a mad woman possessed.

Now that I know what I'm supposed to be doing, it just flows so well, like it's just meant to be.

This process reminds me of two favourite films. One is Arrival where Amy Adam's character sees a glimpse of her future, involving a book she hasn't yet written, and the other is Pan's Labyrinth where the character Ophelia is given a book with blank pages, but when she opens it later alone, the words begin to appear on the page. I feel goosebumps rise on my arms. This feels like something I'm destined to do and I'm so excited to be doing it.

It's now 9 months later and I've had some ups and downs during that time, some dry periods where I just didn't feel inspired, some chapters were so hard to write I couldn't face them and left the project aside for weeks on end. But I made it, Mr Awesome is still here, sometimes I wonder why as the gremlins still like to goad me that I'm overweight, uninteresting and really quite average, but I'm strong enough now to answer them back and say So what? Fuck off who asked you anyway"!

I don't yet know what the future holds for me, I hope I get my happily ever after, God knows I deserve it. Reading this back using the "Read Aloud" function has made me laugh and cry in equal measures. I think whatever life throws at me from now on, I will be strong enough to face it, smart enough to work through it, tough enough to hang on in there.

I'm already brimming with ideas for another book, and perhaps another one after that. People tell me they support me and want to read it. I feel humbled and terrified in equal measures. It feels a bit like throwing my diary into the street for the world to pore over. I know I will get good comments as well as bad ones, that's life though. You can't please everyone. After spending almost seven years trying to please an unpleasable man, and several more trying to live up to the unattainable standards of Watchtower, I'm just going to please me from now on, and those nearest and dearest to me. It's quite liberating. I highly recommend it!

Chapter 23

Hamburg

I wake one cold March morning and look out at the thick blanket of snow which has fallen overnight. It has a pinkish glow to it from the morning sunrise. The childhood saying "Red sky in the morning, Shepherd's Warning" comes to mind. Good job I'm not a Shepherd then. I get up, pop to the loo then it's back to bed to lie for ten minutes in what has become a morning ritual of "Doom Scrolling"

I developed this bad habit around the time of the Covid outbreak and it's one I'm finding hard to shake off. On busy mornings when I don't have time to see what awful things are happening out there in the world I enjoy the blissful ignorance of what is going on, it's never anything good, ever.

The first story I come across this particular morning makes my heart sink. A mass shooting has occurred in Hamburg at a Kingdom Hall. I don't even need to scroll any further than this first line and immediately I know what every JW and Ex JW will respectively be thinking.

As I scroll down the details are sketchy but seven people have been killed and eight have been injured. The lone gunman has committed suicide at the scene. I know as the day goes on, further details will come to light and my heart sinks further and further down. My first thoughts go to the poor, innocent people who lost their lives, their families, the people who survived this incident, the people who witnessed it from neighbouring houses.

My second thought is my Mum, she's in her mid-80's and has dementia, I don't think it's a good idea for her to see this when she turns on her TV. It's been some time since she's physically been to the Kingdom Hall due to being wheelchair bound, but I know this news will upset her. I also shudder with relief that I had long ago decided never to set foot in a Kingdom Hall ever again. I wonder how many people on the inside might be thinking similar thoughts? Will there be a mass Exodus of frightened PIMO's? I quickly text my Sister to convey my thoughts and she messages back to say Thanks for thinking of her but she already saw it on the news last night. She then adds "Sadly, it's gonna happen" she then changes the subject to the weather.

I feel sick to my stomach. She's so blasé. Jehovah's Witnesses have been heavily indoctrinated for some years now with dramatic video productions which show simulations of what Armageddon might look like. All of them have the same theme. Men in black riot gear, heavily armed, coming at them with the intention of killing them. I don't remember exactly when this began but my first recollection of it is the infamous "Bunker Video" where a group of JW's are hiding out in "Brother Brown's" basement, reading scriptures and telling stories to pass the time as the masked men search the streets for any witnesses so they can kill them. They believe this because for some years now, they have applied scriptures from the Bible book of Daniel, deemed by many scholarly experts to be a fake, using them to have a secondary prophetic meaning regarding the end times we supposedly live in today. In the Prophecy there is a King of the North who JW's attribute to be Russia and its allies, spearheaded by Vladimir Putin, in a similar fashion to Adolf Hitler leading the Nazi party to eradicate ethnic and religious groups.

They believe that their lovely, loving, caring God Jehovah, will "put it into the minds" of men to attack their religion and eventually all the people connected to it. They believe a day will come when every witness on the planet will have to face these men in black. Once everyone is rounded up and cornered, the lovely, loving, caring Jehovah will use this as an opportunity to show his almightiness by wiping out every single person on the face of the planet who isn't a Jehovah's Witness. Not just the men in black, innocent people who are nothing to do with any of this. Women, children, babies, animals will get consumed in the crossfire too as anyone who's ever read the old testament knows, animals are completely expendable.

After I bounce back from my initial disgust at my Sister's response to this horrendous tragedy, I feel sorry for her. She's so deeply indoctrinated she lives in a wee bubble where she thinks this is something that's likely to become a monthly, weekly and eventually daily occurrence. The fear mongering videos have done their intended job on her. She feels this is just more proof that the end that's been right around the corner for over 100 years is now about to present itself to the world.

I've tried to wake her up, but the truth is you can't wake someone up if they're not ready to hear it, if they don't want to hear it. It's a sad truth but much like an alcoholic who can't stop drinking until they reach rock bottom and want to, a JW can't wake up unless they have doubts, questions, a curious mind to seek out the answers to them if they feel the Watchtower's aren't satisfactory and above all else a bravery to go against the grain. Jehovah's Witnesses are told they mustn't look to outside sources for information on ANY subject whatsoever. Everything they need to know is micromanaged within the JW website and literature. If you feel the need to look for answers out with this arrangement, there's something wrong with you and your on a slippery slope!

If you're not against the men in black you immediately default to being on their side and worthy of destruction even if you've done nothing to deserve it. My Sister is 30 years in and she is making sure as sure can be, that she doesn't listen to anything that might open her mind to the possibility everything she's being spoon fed is designed to keep her under the Watchtower Mind Control Department.

I've tried a few different techniques, some more subtle than others, to raise questions and provoke her rational thinking abilities. She admitted to me once in a moment of rare honesty, that she also didn't like the sound of Director Dave's Paradise Cities, being assigned where to live even if it doesn't fit the ideal of "Paradise" you have been sold for half your adult life. We were promised Pandas and log cabins, all of a sudden Pointy Stick Dave is telling us we need to toe the line and do as we're told if we're assigned to the New World concrete jungle. I try to use this as an avenue to open up a discussion but I see it in her eyes immediately that she's let a doubt slip out and she's now panicking that she's committed a sin! She might have to go to the thought police Elders and confess that she not only thought something contrary to what she was told to think, but she confessed it to me, an apostate!!

Shortly after, she tells me we can no longer have any form of discussion on anything based on the Bible or religion. She's clearly been given a yellow card and warned to treat me with extreme caution. I'm only allowed to talk about Mum, family matters, gardening and the weather and because I've turned my back on the true God she can't be close to me anymore. It sucks, but I know this is her indoctrination talking, so I try not to let it get to me. I'm potentially her enemy now. Now I've finally come out and said out loud that I think it's all a scam and a mind control cult and I don't ever want a part of it. Until you say those words out loud, a JW will always think there is hope to convert you someday.

I resume scrolling, it's only a short article but my gut feeling is this is an aggrieved apostate who has done this. I wonder how he was able to gain access, first of all to a firearm, as JW's are not supposed to enjoy shooting as it's classed as being a "Lover of violence". My next query is how did he get access to the hall as all meetings have "security" in the form of usually at least two, sometimes more, Brothers subtly guarding the entrance or lobby, specifically trained to look for potential threats and head them off, escorting and ejecting potentially dangerous or troublesome people from the building if need be. My heart sinks as far down as it can go. It's one thing to harbour grief, anger, frustration and resentment for all the years you lose as a JW indoctrinate, years where you are gaslit, closely monitored, controlled and micromanaged. It's a normal process to feel lost, empty, depressed, hopeless and even despair as your entire belief system begins to come apart.

If you pick too much at an annoying loose thread you could risk the whole garment coming unravelled. This is what it's like to wake up. You find an answer to a question outside of where you're allowed to look, so you have another question, that gets answered and before you know it you're sitting surrounded by a lifetime's worth of debunked theories and asking yourself "What do I believe now?" "What do I do now?" It's a tough thing to go through, breaking down all of the childhood indoctrination and examining each teaching one by one until you feel like you're a blank canvas ready to reshape your view of God, the world and everything else.

Normal people ride this emotional rollercoaster and with the right support, come out the other side stronger, wiser, more appreciative of life and the time they have left once they have grieved properly for all that time they can never reclaim.

Sadly, not everyone has access to this support and not everyone who leaves has normal mental health. As much as I hate that word "Normal" the bottom line is that normal people don't get armed to the eyeballs and take out their issues on innocent worshippers.

As the day goes on, I read several updated articles and my suspicions are confirmed. It's a former worshipper who's committed this heinous act. He either left on bad terms, or was disfellowshipped. He shot through the windows into the Kingdom Hall prior to entering it, perhaps to cause maximum victim casualties before anyone could intervene. It's a long standing joke amongst Ex JW's that many if not most Kingdom Halls don't have windows. This one clearly did. I don't think anyone is going to make a joke about that anymore.

My phone pings regularly throughout the day, the Ex JW community is aghast, messages expressing deep sympathies are everywhere to be seen. The Apostate channels I'm subscribed to ping me notifications. Everyone is reeling at what has happened. The strong faithed JW's like my sister, will react with comments such as "Oh that's so sad, but it just goes to show we need the end now more than ever!"

They will offer up prayers for the families but at the same time they will be praying for their lovely, loving, caring God Jehovah to come take his vengeance, anytime soon will do.

This is a really heavy blow to the Ex JW community. Nobody wants to think that carrying the title apostate or Ex JW tars them with the same brush as an extremist murderer.

I'm a straightforward person, it seems to me the sensible thing would be for both communities to be united in their sadness over this tragic event. But if I know anything about the subject by now, it's that the Hateful ~~Eight, Ten,~~ Nine will be having a board meeting as I type to discuss when they will do a press release, what it will contain, and what spin to put on it to enhance the persecution complex and fear mongering of the members. Some of whom might be having doubts or thinking of leaving, and to keep that leash of control as tight as possible around everyone else.

A few days later more details come to light, it seems someone sent an anonymous letter to the Police expressing their concern about the killer's mental health and the fact he owned a firearm. The Police visited and found the gun safely locked away as it should be and the potential killer to be, friendly and cooperative. They found no grounds under which to seize the firearm. Fair play to whoever sent that report. They tried and unfortunately due to the way gun ownership laws are set up, there was no reasonable cause to take the gun away. Such a waste of innocent lives by this one mistake made!

I keep reading and discover the killer self-published a book all about God, Jesus and the Devil not long before his death. I search for the book as in one news report it says he left the congregation on bad terms due to the publication of this book. Immediately on seeing an image of the book cover I can see why. It's a silver book with an almost identical type set as the "Silver Sword" or New World Translation of the Bible commonly used by JW's.

This in itself without even opening the cover to read the contents would be a disfellowshipping offence and considered to be blasphemous to try to copy Watchtower Publications in any way.

I can't control my curiosity and attempt to find the book to either use the "search inside" function to get an overview of its theme or some more information. You all know by now I need answers, enquiring minds need to know more than what's written, I need the back story, to read between the lines. The publication has been pulled from every site where it was previously available. Rightly so really. Someone who commits such a grievous act shouldn't be allowed any more air time.

I know more facts will come to light in time, for now I just feel immense sadness for everyone affected by this. This seems like a very sombre note on which to end this book, but I've already added this additional chapter to the original list I saw so clearly in my mind's eye. If I add more, will the book ever be finished? My journey has now come to a fork where I want to put everything that's happened to me firmly behind me and move in a new, positive direction. My mind has been reeling all afternoon, in the way it usually ruminates once I've experienced the waves of initial emotion. I always come back to the same thought every time. "What can I do to help? What can I do to make a difference?" I don't know yet what or how, but I have to do something, even if it's just to keep tapping away in the present and hope that this reaches and resonates with someone out there in the future.

This chapter is dedicated to those who lost their lives on March 10th 2023 and their families.

Glossary of JW Terminology

- **Adamic Sin** – The concept that Adam and Eve sinned and as we are all their offspring, we have inherited their sin.

- **Annointed** - A person who believes they have been personally called by God to serve him. They believe when they die they go straight to heaven to rule with Jesus and the rest of the 144,000.

- **Apostate** - An abandonment or renunciation of a person's religious beliefs.

- **Apply Yourself** - Work harder doing free labour for Watchtower

- **Babylon the Great** - Watchtower's nickname for all "false" religions other than Jehovah's Witnesses, which they believe will soon be destroyed.

- **Bethel** - JW Headquarters, taken from the Hebrew Word meaning House of God. It's interesting to note that the literal translation is Bet-El or House of El, not House of Jehovah.

- **Bethelite** - A baptised JW man or married JW couple who live at Bethel and work there, almost for free, except for a very meagre personal allowance.

- **Brother / Sister - The name all JW's refer to each other by. Brother being for male members, Sister for female.**

- **Brother Russell - Charles Taze Russell, generally regarded to be the founding father of the JW religion and first president of the Watchtower Society.**

- **Circuit Overseer - Specially appointed Elders who travel around various circuits of congregations of JW's and are responsible for tasks including appointing of Elders, giving talks and spending time with various congregation members as they rely on them for free housing during their week long visits.**

- **Congregation - Individual groups of Jehovah's Witnesses who meet together at a place of worship called a Kingdom Hall. These lowest level members are often referred to as the "Rank and File" JW and the "Worldwide Work" is supported largely by their voluntary donations.**

- **Dedication - When a JW child, or adult decides to dedicate their life to serving Watchtower Society and is then baptised.**

- **Disassociation - The act of formally announcing, or sending a letter announcing your wish to no longer be associated with JW religion.**

- **Disfellowshipping** - When an unrepentant sinner is removed from the congregation or a person deemed to be unrepentant by means of a Judicial Committee.

- **Elder** - Men who are appointed from Ministerial Servants to a higher position where they are responsible for congregational governance, running congregation meetings, giving talks and dispensing discipline amongst members including Judicial committees, marking and disfellowshipping.

- **Faithful Slave** - Taken from Matthew 24:45 This is the name the Governing Body give to themselves even though Jesus was speaking in a parable.

- **Fading** - The process JW's who wake up go through when they discreetly stop attending as many meetings, or move, change congregations or even countries to attempt to quietly vanish from active service in the hope their families wont shun them.

- **Field Service / Field Ministry** - The term JW's use for the time they spend knocking on doors, standing at literature carts, writing letters and any other form of preaching.

- **Governing Body** - The nine male "anointed" leaders of Watchtower Society who make decisions governing the rules and regulations of all JW's worldwide as well as real estate development decisions.

- Great Tribulation - The brief time period JW's believe will occur shortly before Armageddon, during which no more preaching will take place, anyone not a JW is hereafter doomed to destruction and the world will be shaken by dramatic events and "signs"

- Headship Arrangement - Misogynistic arrangement where the husband of the house is superior to his wife, or an adult son might be viewed as superior to his mother if no other male is present. Women have to be quiet and do as they're told. In some instances they must wear a Nora Batty style head scarf in order to be allowed to preach to men.

- Heavenly Hope - According to Watchtower's interpretation of Revelation 7:4 only 144,000 humans will go to heaven to rule with Jesus over the earth. JW's who believe they are one of this special tribe call themselves Annointed. Only anointed men can serve as Governing Body members. Women can be anointed but are not allowed to be a Governing Body member.

- H.L.C - Hospital Liaison Committee, set up to ensure JW's who have to have any form of surgery or medical treatment, do not break their no blood vow.

- Jehovah's Hand - JW's apply this to anything favourable which happens, alluding to the fact Jehovah intervenes in things which benefit Watchtower in some way.

- Judicial Committee - A group of 3 or more men who set up a disciplinary meeting or meetings with someone accused of, or admitting to a sin.

- Kingdom Hall - Meeting place for JW worship. Usually built using free labour supplied by volunteer congregation members and funded by donations made by JW members.

- Marking - The process whereby Elders "mark" someone who's conduct is improper in some way, but not severe enough to lead to disfellowshipping. Marked persons may have privileges removed or be subject to a soft form of shunning such as not being invited to social gatherings etc.

- Ministerial Servant - The first position of responsibility in the Watchtower hierarchy which is always filled by men, some as young as in their late teens. Duties include handling microphones, sound equipment, Bible reading and saying prayers.

- **Ministry** - The name given to any preaching work JW's do where they count time on their activities.

- **New Light** - Taken from the scripture at Proverbs 4:18 JW's apply this term anytime they change or modify a doctrine, claiming that God is shining the light on things so they have a new and clear understanding of it, when in reality often doctrine is changed completely, then years later changed back again. Or changed back and forth multiple times. Basically it is a free pass for Watchtower to change scriptural understanding to suit their current narrative.

- **Old Light** - Old teachings which are often dispensed with and anyone promoting or continuing them can be labelled an apostate and risks disfellowshipping, even though these doctrines come from Watchtower publications themselves.

- **Pioneer** - Someone who commits to a certain amount of preaching every month, usually 70 hours, although this may have changed at the time of going to print.

- **PIMI** - The first of the three phases of "Waking Up" from JW indoctrination. It stands for Physically in, Mentally in and means the person is a believing JW who is attending meetings and engaging in the ministry.

- **PIMO** - The second phase where a JW begins to doubt, wake up or lose their belief but due to the fear of their family or entire social circle shunning them, they feel compelled to continue pretending they still believe and attending meetings and/or ministry. It stands for Physically in, mentally out. Many PIMO's lead extremely exhausting "Double lives" and this can take a real toll on their mental health.

- **POMO** - The final stage of exiting the JW religion, it stands for Physically out, Mentally out and refers to someone who has fully left the organisation. The most rewarding of the three stages often comes at a great sacrifice and many POMOS lose their family support system.

- **Privileges** - The name given to roles assigned within the congregation such as opening and closing with prayer, leading meetings, giving talks, being a ministerial servant, being an Elder or if you are a woman, being allowed to clean the Kingdom Hall toilets or hoover/mop the floors.

- **Ransom Sacrifice** - The belief that Jesus is the son of God and came to Earth to offer his perfect human life as a ransom to reclaim what Adam and Eve lost for humanity.

- **Resurrection** - The JW belief that everyone who dies before Armageddon will be eligible for a resurrection into a paradise Earth with the exception of those deemed too evil for one, such as Judas Iscariot. JW's believe that everyone who dies at Armageddon remains eternally dead, which by now you are probably thinking what? How is that fair? But it's what they believe. Fed up yet? I feel your pain, it's exhausting just writing this list but it must be done!

· **Satan** - Previously a wonderful angel in heaven who became jealous of the worship Adam and Eve gave to God so he pretended to be a talking snake to entice her to eat the forbidden fruit. JW's believe he and his followers, referred to as Demons, were cast down to Earth in 1914 and this is why the world is in such a mess. Even though we have a huge increase in life expectancy, general living conditions, medical and technological advancements etc

· **Serving where the greed is greater** - Pioneers who want to travel to a foreign country to try to bring more followers into the fold.

· **Shunning** - Taken mostly from the scripture 2 John 1:10 – 11 this is the cruel practice of shunning or refusing to talk to anyone who is disfellowshipped, leaves or disassociates from the JW religion, in particular if you make it known you are an apostate.

· **Spiritual Food** - Taken mostly from the scripture Matthew 24:45 Watchtower use this term to refer to any written or digital media produced by them. This is considered to be the only acceptable reading and viewing material for JW's, for fear they might actually see what is really going on and stop donating their money.

- **Spiritual / Scriptural Warfare** - Watchtower - given permission to lie about anything they see fit to if it serves their purpose. Jesus said to tell the truth but Watchtower are allowed to lie on his and his father's behalf if it advances their aims.

- **Stumbling** - The practice of advertently or inadvertently doing something, perhaps quite minor, to upset or offend another JW who might then lose some of their faith as a result. Yes, this is really how fragile this religion is.

- **The "Truth"** - The self-professed name JW's give to their religion, believing that all other religions in the world are false and part of Babylon the Great.

- **Time (or counting Time)** - The hours JW's spend in the Ministry or Field Service each month.

- **Two Witness Rule** - One of the most shocking of all JW doctrine which requires an allegation of child abuse to have someone other than the accuser witness the crime. In most cases there are no witnesses so it is "Left in Jehovah's hands" and not reported to any authorities.

- **Waking Up** - The process where a JW begins to realise everything they have been told or taught is a lie.

- **Warning Talk** - A talk given by Elders after an accusation or confession of sin has been made or someone has been removed from the congregation. The person is not named in this talk, but everyone in the congregation gets to know what sin they have committed from the nature of the warning talk.

- **Worldly** - Anyone who is not a JW. Often used as a derogatory term to infer Worldly people are evil or inferior.

Recommended Reading / Viewing

I have written the following in the order in which I began watching and reading as I woke up, but feel free to jump in anywhere with whomever you think will help you the most, they are all great in their own unique ways and you will not regret any time spent in the company of any of these authors or content creators.

- Lloyd Evans. Author of the Reluctant Apostate and YouTube video creator. One of the longest standing ex JW activists, most people find Lloyd first, as I did and then branch out from there. His factual and often comedic look at the entire JW culture is not to be missed.

- Raymond Franz. Author of Crisis of Conscience, former Governing Body Member and whistle blower considered by many to be the foremost source for insider JW information on corruption and malpractice. He was a very humble man who has left an amazing legacy.

- Paul Grundy JWFACTS.COM an amazing website with so much information. It took me a long time to get through all of the articles but Paul has such a great way of explaining everything clearly and concisely.

- Barbara Anderson, author of Barbara Anderson Uncensored and WATCHTOWERDOCUMENTS.ORG website. Whistle-blower and reform activist, this wonderful woman, an ex Bethelite could not sit silently and watch as Watchtower Policies covered up countless incidents of child abuse.

- Ali Millar, author of The Last Days and fellow Scottish ex JW activist. This ladies wonderful book made me laugh and cry in equal measures and gave me the final push of inspiration needed to write this book. Thankyou Ali.

- Wally Barnett, YouTube creator JW THOUGHTS. Wally's videos are well researched and often hilarious. He is one of my favourite content creators and I love how interactive he is with his fans. Well done Wally, keep up the good work!

- JEXIT 2020, Riley is a superb YouTube content creator, he produces very thought provoking videos on subjects often not covered by other creators and is also very interactive with his fans.

- **THE TRUTH HURTS, Harrison** is a wonderful YouTube content creator who presents his arguments in a very straightforward and logical way. He also has some pretty awesome comedy/parody videos which are well worth checking out.

- Last but not least, **GOATLIKE PERSONALITY,** YouTube creator who has a very sad story of his mistreatment whilst in the JW religion but has now found happiness outside the organisation as a goat farmer and reform activist. You will laugh, you will cry, he will spur you to action. His videos are simply comedy genius!

At the time of my final edit of this book, prior to going to print, I have also discovered the excellent scholar Eric Michael Wilson BEROEANS.NET and feel this author and youtube content creator deserves a mention. It is often assumed that upon exiting the JW religion, most people go on to become atheists, however if you find yourself, as I did, not quite ready to abandon Jesus, this is a meaty, well researched and fascinating book which examines scriptures and allows them to unfold naturally, without the tainted bias of the JW indoctrination. I'm currently three quarters of the way through reading his book SHUTTING THE DOOR TO THE KINGDOM OF GOD and can highly recommend it if you want something thought provoking to really get your teeth into!

Of course there are hundreds more, some of whom I have on my seemingly endless "To Watch / Read" list so apologies to anyone who feels missed out, these are simply the people I found most helpful on my personal journey. I hope you find some or all of them helpful too.

About this Book

This is the part where I'm supposed to tell you all about what made me write this book but the truth is it was a cheaper option than therapy!

Many times I questioned every single word and hit the delete button on whole paragraphs and chapters more times than I care to remember, but I felt I needed to write it. As you'll remember from an earlier chapter, I have had some very significant, almost prophetic dreams during my lifetime and this book featured heavily in one of them. They say there is a book in everyone.

This is mine.

I truly hope you have enjoyed reading it.

<u>About Me</u>

This is the part where I'm supposed to tell you some blurb about me, but the truth is I've already poured my heart and soul into every page, you've read a summary of my entire life up until now. You will have already formed your opinion of who you think I am. I have made many mistakes in my life but all of them led me to where I am now, which is in a much better place both mentally and emotionally.

The only thing I know for certain is that my journey doesn't end here, neither does yours. The moment we close the cover against this final page a whole new, fresh chapter begins. We can all choose whether to let the chapters of the past shape us, define us, or use them as a valuable learning tool to cope with the uncharted sea of empty pages ahead - just waiting for an exciting new story to be written upon them!

It is my greatest hope that this book might inspire and embolden others to share their own stories. To stand up and be counted. Reading the books and following the advice of the authors contained in the Suggested Reading section helped give me the push I badly needed to make the dream a reality. I'm just one teeny piece of a huge jigsaw, a sprinter with a baton who must quickly pass it to the next person and so on, until we become a huge sea of voices, starting as a few waves and eventually becoming a deafening roar.

One day, when enough stories have been told, the leaders of religious cults who shirk their accountability for the abuse of children and resultant cover ups, may be forced to change their policies and make better provision for child safeguarding.

If I can contribute to this forward progress, or inspire someone else to do the subject more justice, I'll consider my mission complete.

I would finally like to thank all of my wonderful friends for walking alongside me on this journey, too many to mention, but especially to Sara for always being there, Kym and Nora for helping me with my terrible grasp of the English language and punctuation, Nicci for the tech help, the Ex JW community for their daily, uplifting, un-spiritual food, laughs and moral support and Mr Awesome for putting up with me through thick and thin while I was writing all of this.

To new chapters and new adventures!

"I'll tell you a secret.

Something they don't teach you in your temple.

The Gods envy us.

They envy us because we're mortal, because any moment might be our last. Everything is more beautiful because we're doomed.

You will never be lovelier than you are now. We will never be here again."

-       **Brad Pitt**

Christian Congregation
of Jehovah's Witnesses

1 Kingdom Way, West Hanningfield, Chelmsford, CM2 8LW Telephone 020 8906 2211

SDD   July 8, 2022

Re: Your Recent Letter

Dear Sister

We are replying to your recent letter in which you ask important questions related to the handling of child abuse allegations by Jehovah's Witnesses. We hope our comments can help answer these for you.

Sister . . . . . . may we sympathise with you over the distressing events you experienced as a vulnerable child. Jehovah God abhors the abuse of children in any form. His view is that children are a sacred trust, an "inheritance." (Psalm 127:3) His purpose has always been for children to be cared for kindly, nurtured in a warm loving family environment, and he set the example on how to do this. (Matthew 3:17) Sadly, situations have developed in some families that Jehovah did not purpose or condone.

In like manner, Jehovah's people view child sexual abuse as a gross sin and heinous crime. Like you, we wholeheartedly look forward in faith to a time when such wickedness will no longer occur. (Psalm 37:8-11; Isaiah 65:17) The protection of children is of utmost concern and importance to all Jehovah's Witnesses. **In every case,** victims, their parents, and anyone else have the absolute right to report an accusation of child abuse to the authorities **at any time.**—*Enjoy Life Forever!* Endnote 7.

We note your concerns regarding the elders' role in reporting child abuse accusations to the authorities. The document, *Jehovah's Witnesses' Scripturally Based Position on Child Protection* explains our policy. It can be downloaded from www.jw.org. (Go to Newsroom>Legal Developments>Legal Resources>Downloadable Information Packets.) Point 5 states: "When elders learn of an accusation of child abuse, they immediately consult with the branch office of Jehovah's Witnesses to ensure compliance with child abuse reporting laws. (Romans 13:1) *Even if the elders have no legal duty* to report an accusation to the authorities, the branch office of Jehovah's Witnesses will instruct the elders to report the matter if a minor is still in danger of abuse or there is some other valid reason."—Italics ours.

Points 11 and 12 add: "If it is determined that one guilty of child sexual abuse is repentant and will remain in the congregation, restrictions are imposed on the individual's congregation activities. The individual will be specifically admonished by the elders not to be alone in the company of children, not to cultivate friendships with children, or display any affection for children. In addition, elders may inform parents of minors within the congregation of the need to monitor their children's interaction with the individual. A person who has engaged in child sexual abuse does not qualify to receive any congregation privileges or to serve in a position of responsibility in the congregation for decades, if ever.—1 Timothy 3:1-7, 10; 5:22; Titus 1:7."

The subject of child abuse and how it is handled by the Christian congregation is also discussed at length in three study articles that appeared in *The Watchtower* of May 2019. We encourage you to read

SDD July 8, 2022
Page 2

these. Also, mature Christian sisters and congregation elders are ready to provide you with support. Of course, it is entirely your decision, but you may wish to confide in such ones in order to further benefit from Jehovah's loving care.—Isaiah 66:13; 1 Thessalonians 2:7; 4:18.

Continue in your wise course of learning about our great God, Jehovah. (Psalm 37:5-11) Let nothing prevent you from enjoying his close friendship and the peace of mind it brings. (Romans 8:38, 39; Philippians 4:7) And may he bless your efforts as you do this.—James 4:8a.

Please be assured of our warm love and affection.

Your brothers,

Christian Congregation
of Jehovah's Witnesses

Printed in Great Britain
by Amazon

33868653R00188